THE BUDDHA
AT MY TABLE

THE BUDDHA
AT MY TABLE

How I Found Peace in Betrayal and Divorce

Tammy Letherer

SHE WRITES PRESS

Published 2018
Printed in the United States of America
ISBN: 978-1-63152-425-7
978-1-63152-426-4

Library of Congress Control Number: 2018938592

For information, address:
She Writes Press
1569 Solano Ave #546
Berkeley, CA 94707

She Writes Press is a division of SparkPoint Studio, LLC.

For my mother
And for all mothers
who are doing the very best they can

To a Friend

I ask but one thing of you, only one,
That always you will be my dream of you;
That never shall I wake to find untrue
All this I have believed and rested on,
Forever vanished, like a vision gone
Out into the night. Alas, how few
There are who strike in us a chord we knew
Existed, but so seldom heard its tone
We tremble at the half-forgotten sound.
The world is full of rude awakenings
And heaven-born castles shattered to the ground,
Yet still our human longing vainly clings
To a belief in beauty through all wrongs.
O stay your hand, and leave my heart its songs!

—Amy Lowell

Part One

People only see what they are prepared to see.

—Ralph Waldo Emerson

I The Blow

It's the clink of ice against glass that wakes me. I hear my husband, Dave, in the kitchen, a slosh of something being poured, and I look over from where I was dozing on the sofa to see him come into the room with two fingers of amber liquid in a highball. Scotch on the rocks. I sit up. It's not his habit to have a drink alone. In fact, we don't usually have alcohol in the house. But recently, since joining a neighborhood poker group, he's begun discerning between single and double malt scotches and seems to be relishing the good ol' boy status it gives him.

He sets the drink carefully on the dining room table. I turn back to the television show I was watching before I nodded off, called *House*, about a misanthropic medical genius. Dr. House is growling something demeaning to a female doctor. It's his way of being adorable, and because he's brilliant and saves people's lives, he gets a pass on basic civility.

"Is your show almost done?" Dave asks. "Can you come sit at the table?"

"Why?" It's drafty in the house, and there's a bare Christmas tree propped in the corner. The scent of pine adds to my sense of being exposed to the elements and makes me want to burrow back under the flannel throw blanket over my knees.

He doesn't answer. I get up, flip off the TV, and move to join him at the table. He has his drink and a piece of paper in front of him.

"I have to tell you something and I want you to let me get through it without interrupting me because it will be hard for me."

I nod, but my mouth goes dry. He's been fired! And right before Christmas! But in a nanosecond, that thought is rejected. Dave was a freelance writer for many years and would not be worried to be back on his own.

"Number one," he says, looking down at his paper. "About ten years ago, when we'd been married a couple of years, I had an affair. It was someone in radio, someone I knew from being in the band, and I ended it pretty quickly."

My heart skids. I silently repeat the words *ten years ago,* and *I ended it.* Before I can process this, Dave goes on.

"Number two: I've been using escorts on my business trips."

No, no, no. Flashes of soulless, transactional sex assault me but I refuse to look. I stare straight ahead, not blinking, not breathing.

"You know what escorts are, don't you?" He adds this patiently, almost gently, as if I'm a child. Or maybe he's only reacting to the incomprehension in my face. The absurdity of his question short circuits something in my brain. *Do I know what escorts are?* I feel myself sinking to the floor, reaching for the hardwood as it slides eerily away from me.

I'm on my knees, gripping my thighs. "I'm going to be sick," I say, and begin peeling off my sweatshirt. Dave doesn't move, and I know there's more. "Say it! Just say it!"

"Three weeks ago, when I was in Las Vegas, I met someone."

Dizzy, I scramble on the floor in a sort of stunned crab-crawl. White-hot, blinding terror envelops me like a blanket: This must be what death feels like. Dave does nothing to help me and that's when, for a brief moment, I wonder if I ever existed.

When I come back into my body (Moments later? Minutes?) Dave is talking, saying something about moving upstairs. I don't understand. How could he move upstairs? Our tenant lives there. I hear the words *committed father*. What is he talking about? What about me?

His explanations are like blades pinning me to a wall: He spent twelve hours with a woman named Allison in Las Vegas. He's in love. She lives in Texas. He wants to visit her. He will ask our tenant to leave. He will move into the upstairs apartment. He would like to *"wrap things up"* with me in four weeks. He is going to leave the house now because he needs to call Allison. She's waiting to hear from him.

I hear him walk out the door and panic overtakes me. I get up, pacing and flailing my arms, trying to feel my hands and feet. I'm alone in the house, and my children are sleeping in their beds, and I can't faint or scream or lose it. I begin to cry but it's more of a moan. I grab my phone and call my friend and neighbor Abigail. No answer. I try my college friend. No answer. My brother. No answer. I consider calling my mother, but I know she'll be sleeping, and I can't wake her with this. I don't know how much time passes before I finally realize another crushing truth: I have no one to call but Dave.

"You have to come home," I say when he finally answers. "Please come home. Don't leave me here alone."

I wait by the front window, half hidden behind the Christmas tree, the pine needles poking my shoulder every time I breathe. Dave needs to bring the ornaments and lights up from the basement. *Dave needs to. . . . Dave needs to. . . .* The words replay in my head until he gets back. By then I've found a way to frame this: Dave needs me to help him. Dave is having a crisis and it's up to me to pull him back from the ledge. I go wash my face and brush my teeth, moving like an automaton until, minutes later, we're lying beside each other in bed. It's a habit of twenty years, and disrupting it doesn't occur to me. I stare at the ugly ceiling fixture I've been wanting to replace with a small chandelier, an idea that now seems misguided and theatrical.

"What about the kids?"

Dave seems genuinely surprised, as if he'd forgotten them.

"Do you want them to be from a broken family?"

He uses the word *resilient*. "If we're friendly, they'll be fine."

I glimpse the role he wants me to play: Tammy will go away quietly, with a smile on her face. He makes a point of saying that he's not like my dad. He'll be a good parent. I want to remind him that the pain I feel about my father continues because he never acknowledged any wrongdoing. He left my family without looking back, never caring how I was personally affected. I want to warn Dave that he'll have to put honesty and remorse before resilience. But this seems too much to bite off just now, so I scramble for the correct words. I only need to make the right points, in the right order, to lead him out of this. I think of a TV show I saw once about divorce, where a therapist went to the couple's house to give them a reality check on what they were about to do. They had to sit in front of photos of their kids and deliver the news. In the show, this simple role play was upsetting enough to bring reconciliation.

Carefully, I ask, "What will you tell them?" My words are weighted but I can't tell if he catches my emphasis. I mean to say that *he* will tell them and they will know that this is *his* choosing.

He says nothing.

"Have you thought about what it will be like not living with them?"

Tears thicken his voice. "No, no, I don't want that!"

Okay, then. I can do this. I can restore his reason. I won't allow my children to be products of divorce, to feel the confusion, anger, and self-blame that I felt as a teenager. I've been handed a divine task, a chance to do things differently than my parents. To be better. Dave has always said he wants us to be extraordinary, so this is our gift. We'll take a devastating event and rise above it. What an example we'll be.

Silently I take his hand, imagining our children here in the room with us, reminding Dave of his duty. I'll let this sink in while I remain a loving, solid presence.

I will be our rock. And like a rock, I won't think. I won't feel.

2 The Dream

Every year Dave and I host a dinner for our friends the Saturday after Thanksgiving. This year I was especially excited, thanks to my newly-spiffed living room. As a long time interior design junkie, I had labored valiantly to bring some style to that room. I'd hand-painted a beautiful oak cabinet I found in the alley, upholstered an armchair a friend didn't want, bartered for a sofa. But no matter how much HGTV I watched, I couldn't get my *Design on a Dime* to look anything but chintzy. So I splurged by spending four hundred dollars on a team of home staging experts. Using my own things, they spent four hours working magic. When I stepped into my new room, I was stunned. They did *that* with my old stuff? It was, finally, a look as polished as what I had long imagined.

As our friends gathered, I took pictures of everyone chatting in the living room—the lighting was perfect, the seating ample!—and I was so proud and pleased of the tableau Dave and I had created. When we moved to the dining room and began our dinner with each of us giving thanks, Dave was the last to go. He stood at the head of the table and raised his glass.

"I'm grateful for my beautiful wife," he said. Then he added that he was also thankful for Eckhart Tolle's book *A New Earth*. I'd read it recently and was so inspired that I'd urged it on Dave. Since he doesn't share my self-help or spiritual interests, I was surprised when he picked it up. I was also surprised that he included it in his toast. He didn't discuss it with me, so I was unaware that it had moved him. But how encouraging! I even went so far as to imagine a new era for the two of us, one where Dave might embrace some sort of spirituality and want to discuss life's Big Questions with me.

Days after our glowing soiree, I was happily planted in my fresh digs, watching television, while Dave put the kids to bed. This was my break time, when I got to hand the reins to him. Dave enjoyed reading bedtime stories, which was great, except that he often fell asleep while reading; meantime, I sat waiting for him to join me. There were conversations, some mundane, some self-centered, that I saved to share with him. Yet by the time he came down I was often too groggy or hooked into a favorite show. *It will wait* had become all too common.

That night, even the irascible Dr. House couldn't keep me awake. I first heard the creak of Dave's foot on the wooden stair. Or was it the glug of liquid? No, that's right—it was the unlikely pop of ice in Dave's glass. I saw the piece of paper in his hand and the fold marks on it that told me it had lived in his pocket. He stood at the table and placed his glass down so carefully.

"Can you come sit at the table?" That's what he said.

On Thanksgiving morning I was driving with Dave and the kids through the cornfields and flat land of northern Illinois. Prairie land, it's called, though to me those words have a forced nostalgia. Prairie is Laura Ingalls Wilder's domain—tall flowing grasses, gingham dresses and sunbonnets, wildflowers and grazing cows. Our minivan, disentangled at last from Chicago traffic, passed industrial complexes, billboards and water towers, fallow, snow-covered fields. The kids were briefly diverted counting the line of incoming airplanes descending toward O'Hare airport. After that, April, our three-year-old daughter, set her sights on counting horses. That tally, even stretched over two hours, took one hand, and she fell asleep halfway through.

For the twentieth year in a row, we were headed for a table loaded with turkey, ham, more varieties of bread and potatoes than Betty Crocker could count, and a Jell-O mold. For dessert there were palm-sized cookies shaped like turkeys and iced with soft pillows of whipped sugar. Americana. It was family tradition, unsurprising and predictable, as comfortable as the way your own cheek rests in the curve of your hand when you're allowed to put your elbows on the table, suggesting boredom, maybe, but look how the pieces fit!

We fit, my Midwestern, middle-income, minivan-clad clan. Dave and I were proud to be urbanites. We were both creatives—marketing copywriters by day, but by night Dave wrote songs and played music, and I dreamed of writing books. We made a beeline to Chicago after attending Big Ten schools, eager to soak up culture and diversity and micro-brewed beer. We'd become a bit puffed up, honestly, fairly dripping with self-satisfaction. Holidays were like washing onto a beach. We dried out, dwindling down to spiny shells, neither more remarkable than the other. Two days of this and we risked extinction if we didn't throw ourselves back into our life.

For me it was a life that revolved around my kids. I'd spent the previous day with my son Jed's class on a field trip to a writing and literacy program in Chicago called Open Books. On the bus, Jed sat beside another boy, but they didn't talk. I was watchful and curious, wondering. *Does he have friends? Do the kids like him? Why isn't he participating?* I worried that my own quietness had cursed Jed with a gene that made it hard for him to be one of the crowd. During the presentation he was like a noodle, clinging to me, and I was embarrassed. The kids were asked to write about a loved one. Jed didn't show me his work, but when they asked someone to share, he startled me by raising his hand. He said he chose to write about me. He stood and told the other kids that I'm good at jokes, smart at math, and five feet tall. None of this is true, but isn't poetic license beautiful?

He also told everyone that I'm a writer and that, more than anything, made me cringe. It took me thirteen years to finish my first book—a novel called, coincidentally enough, *Hello Loved Ones*—between having three kids, moving three times, renovating a one-hundred-year-old two-flat, and owning, growing, and selling my own business. Lately I'd been discouraged by the tedious and time-consuming process of looking for an agent. The last blow to my confidence had come at a writers' conference I attended where I had the opportunity to pitch my book to several New York agents. One of them—she couldn't have been older than twenty-five—told me bluntly that no one was interested in reading a story set in 1968. It made me want to give up. But that field trip, with its focus on writers and books, has had me thinking again about my novel and my dream of having it published. *Author, novelist, writer.* I love the ring of those words. But the characters that were once so real to me have been shelved to make room for the living, breathing members of my family.

My writing has to wait.

I offered to take the wheel first, and by the time we neared Rockford and rounded the exit ramp past Magic Waters Theme Park, everyone, including Dave, was asleep. I felt slightly bereft. I was still attached to a seventies mentality that believed road trips were a time for rounds of "slug bug" or show tune sing-alongs. No, that wasn't my childhood, but I hadn't stopped hoping. After an hour of listening to my daughter's stuffy-nosed snore and wondering how long my oldest son, Logan, could sleep with his neck squashed at that angle, my cell phone rang. It was my older brother, Bryan. I asked what he was doing and he said he was going to spend Thanksgiving with our dad.

There was a pause.

I'm not sure when my family landscape changed. Growing up, there were definite territories. Me, my mom, and my siblings on one side, my dad across the Great Divide. My dad was the type who seemed . . . I would say *uncomfortable* with fatherhood. He was not a *committed father*, like Dave. When my parents divorced, I was sixteen, and I've had little contact with him since. I lived my early adulthood waiting to be handed a map to Dadland, or better, to be rescued by a search party, while my brother apparently forged over on his own. I imagined the two of them making historic discoveries together, killing a fatted calf, mugs raised high, bonding in a way that requires Y chromosomes.

I felt again the familiar sense of being left out, but I recovered enough to chat with Bryan. When I hung up, something happened in my chest. A pressure built and I began to cry in what I call the *movie star way*, one or two tears slipping elegantly down my cheek. I saw myself as if through a lens. I only wished I had a director to explain the scene. I'm one who likes a script, something to tell me how to act. But there was no director, only me having a sad, private moment in a carload of people. I felt surprised, indignant, betrayed, hurt. There was a petulance rising. *I want a dad! Why can't I have a dad?*

Why was that moment significant? The phone call came. I heard my brother's plans. I hung up. I felt something. I cried. Total elapsed time? Five minutes, max. Maybe this was normal for most people, but my normal was a little more complex. I liked to take a feeling and push it into a capsule, then send it whizzing through an elaborate, intricate scaffold constructed over many years, consisting of shoots and trapdoors, dead ends and derailments, like a marble dropping and twisting while I waited, never knowing where it would land. This time, though, the marble hit a catapult (who put *that* there?), and in one fell swoop it shot up and out. It was free. Like a psychic Heimlich, something came unstuck, and I was clear. I was having, at last, what my therapist has described as an emotion in *real time*.

I considered waking Dave, but what would I say? *Boo-hoo, I'm sad about my dad.* I'd sound like a five-year-old (or a Dr. Seuss rhyme), a regression that made sense if you were into, you know, the whole therapy thing. But Dave was not. We were on the way to his intact family who lived in a state of abiding Sameness: same food, same traditions, same house, same small town. All the dysfunction was reserved for my family.

Besides, Dave already saw me as overly analytical. I sensed a rolling of the eyes over my continuing family dramas and my need to understand them. Certainly I was guilty of some navel-gazing. But one payoff was Dave himself. He was solid as the day was long, opposite in all ways from my father. I'd chosen well, and this was one thing I gave thanks for on that day—silently, because Dave's family was not religious, a trait I decided long ago to see as refreshing and forward-thinking. So no prayers were said, but I was grateful, as always, that Dave was my dream of him.

3 The Pieces

Webster's Dictionary defines the word "moment" as an indefinitely short period of time. Also, as a definite period or stage. I love that contradiction and the fact that both are true. There are happy moments, defining moments, transcendent moments. Dave has spoken often of the moment of our first son's birth. A stubborn breech baby, Logan arrived through a planned cesarean section. I worried about Dave's presence in the operating room because he has a strange relationship with blood. A small amount, from a cut or gash, will launch his vasovagal response, and he'll feel faint. But large scale gore, especially the movie kind, doesn't bother him, nor did it faze him to see the doctors pull out my insides and set them on my stomach before extracting the baby. He likes to say that he saw me gutted. I wonder how a person can look at another person's insides and not have some consideration for the heart that beats that blood.

I also wonder how it's possible to be in the middle of something and at the same time watching from a distance. I felt that way during the C-section. My head was like a balloon drifting away from what I knew to be my body. I barely managed to croak out a warning to the anesthesiologist that I couldn't swallow, and if she hadn't eased up on the dials, I'm convinced I would have disappeared in a puff of smoke. Yet as surreal as that surgery felt, I was anchored by the promise of my son. His arrival made it all worthwhile. Now I can't conceive of any eventual joy. I feel fractured, as if pieces have fallen with such force that I'll never find them. Again, I imagine my life as a movie and this is where the film comes dangerously close to breaking. It flickers, flashing segments that are interspersed with white static and whirring blankness:

I stand on my friend Abigail's doorstep. It's early morning, just hours after The Blow. Her children and husband must be there getting ready for their day, but I don't see them. There's a black leather sofa. I'm crying. And cold. So cold I can't stop shivering. There's a blanket. Abigail listens, stunned. She's weathered some harsh storms herself, and this has made her unshakable. She steadies me with immediate practicalities. A cup of tea. A few sleeping pills. Have I left a message for my therapist? I don't want to leave her house. I'm very afraid. I see already the blight I carry, like a cancer. I see how I will be feared, set apart, avoided. But not by Abigail. She sits quietly and lets me be.

I'm in bed. It's 4:30 a.m. I'm crying. Dave turns and puts his arms around me. I'm relieved that there is still comfort there. How much longer will that be the case? He may soon be gone. How soon? I know I should force him out, but I can't bear the finality of that. I feel his breath on my ear. He says he has an idea. He would like for each of us to say something about the other that we appreciate. He wants to do this every morning before we greet the kids and every evening when he's in the car on his way home from work. I'm surprised but tell myself that he's *trying*. But trying *what*? I don't know what he wants or what's going to happen. I don't know if this is his attempt to create a pleasant environment so he can leave me with less guilt, or if he really wants to heal something with me. Whatever his reasons,

I agree, and he begins. He's emotional and struggling. He's grateful, he says, that I have been—I don't catch the word he uses and it's *so* important. Is it *good*? I have been *good* about all this? Reasonable? He says he appreciates that I didn't lose it and I want to interject, *how would you know*? Sure, I didn't rage or shriek or lunge at him with balled fists, but only because I'm still reeling. I've lost my claim to a happy marriage; lost the pride that came with being smarter or luckier than so many others; lost the separation between me and "those women" who must be, somehow, to blame for their cheating husbands; lost respect for the father of my children—the list of things I've lost seems endless. But I don't say any of this. Dave thanks me for talking to him and for being loving. I wonder what he expected of me. I wonder who the hell he thinks I am.

I schedule an emergency session with my therapist, Walter. I'm basically paying him to listen to me cry, but I would gladly give my last cent for his solid, unflinching presence. I relate Dave's idea to share our appreciation with each other, and Walter says it's a lovely practice in a loving relationship, but a little odd in this case, when Dave is most likely not coming clean. Walter says he's touched by my commitment to my family and marriage, and that if we come through this, and I stay with him, Dave will never be able to thank me enough. This makes me cry even harder. I don't want to be a fucking martyr. I want to believe in love, and I don't see how, if I live to be one hundred, I will ever get that back.

I find Dave sleeping in our bed with the boys asleep beside him, their books still open. I wake my older son, Logan, and help him to bed before carrying Jed, still asleep, to his room. I take a sleeping pill at 9:00 p.m. and sleep hard until 4:30 a.m., a time that is quickly becoming the witching hour, when my demons are most powerful. I wake to the sound of Dave snoring. I lay for awhile, listening, growing more and more indignant. How can he sleep? I know he didn't take a sleeping pill. He never does. Yet I'm certain he's been asleep for hours. The lying, cheating bastard confesses, thereby transferring his load of shit to me, and he sleeps like a baby! When the alarm rings at 6:30 a. m., I don't think I can get up. My head is thick and pounding, and I'm nauseated. I try to work it out; what *exactly* has Dave said? He's had many affairs. He thinks he loves a woman he just met. He wants to move upstairs. But he doesn't want the kids coming from a broken home. What does it mean? Now I do want to rage at him, to grab him and shake him out of his sickening nonchalance. I want to turn his world upside down in an instant and ask him how *resilient* he feels.

I elbow him, hard, and he groans. I ask him what he talked to Allison about when he called her the other night.

He stretches and rolls over to face the ceiling. "She agrees with you that we should have no contact."

"Well, gold star for her!" I snap. "What about you?"

He hesitates, then says that they will probably do that. Somehow I get it out of him that Allison has been in his cell phone contacts under the name Ken. Ken is his boss. I think of all the times I've seen that name, and my stomach lurches. I make it to the bathroom before retching, but nothing comes up. I'm an empty shell.

The subject of telling Dave's parents comes up, and I say I'd like to be present when he calls them, not because I have any idea what to say, but because I want to hear what Dave will say. He agrees, yet when I walk into the basement that night, I find him locked in his office on the phone. There are french doors separating it from the playroom, so I can see him through the glass. He sees my quizzical look, mouths *my mom*, and makes a vague motion that I interpret as *don't worry, everything's fine.* But I am worried. And angry. This is so blatantly the opposite of what we discussed. When he emerges, his attitude is nonchalant, as if it's no big deal. He assures me that he told them the truth, and I finally get to see what he looks like when he lies.

I go to my computer and compose an email to Dave's parents, my in-laws of twelve years. *I know that Dave has told you the news that he met someone recently in Las Vegas and wants a divorce. I want you to know that I love him and am committed to working this out.* I say this because I think it's true. I say it because it has to be true. Because if it's not true, then what?

I'm in an evening yoga class with the woman we call The Yoga Goddess. What am I doing here? Abigail brought me, and I followed like a still-blind kitten, weak and helpless. How can I move my body through poses when the mat is calling me to lie down and curl into myself? Even in this room of mostly strangers, I feel ashamed and embarrassed, as if everyone can see what my husband has done. I don't want anyone to look at me, yet I'm certain everyone is. I burn with humiliation. I'm aware of the dimness of the room and the radiance of the instructor. I love her and hate her too, for being happy and beautiful. My life is over. With each exhale comes the only mantra I can manage: Why? Why? Why?

I'm waiting on my front porch for a friend. We're going to check out a new Montessori program being offered at a public school. Our daughters go to Montessori preschool together, and we've been debating their options for the fall. This open house has been on my calendar for weeks, but today it feels so trivial. I don't bother looking for the questions I've compiled; I know I won't ask any. I'm going simply because I told my friend I would, and I don't know what else to do. Part of me is impressed that I'm soldiering on, getting my kids to school, and keeping appointments. But my armor must show cracks because as soon as I climb into the car she asks what's wrong. I blurt out what happened. All of it. But I don't cry, and for this I'm grateful. I don't know her well enough to dissolve in a puddle on her car seat, especially when she is trying to focus on one of the most challenging tasks facing Chicago parents: public school placement.

At the school, we walk down a long, gray hallway. I touch the lockers along the wall to steady myself. I know my daughter will not get into the program. I know that her life, too, will not be following my best-laid plans.

Dave and I get a session with a therapist recommended by a friend. Her name is Mary, and she's straightforward and practical. After we've told our story, she asks if we are here for marriage therapy or divorce therapy. Neither of us can answer. She advises me to negotiate with Dave. What will it take for him to stay in the marriage? How will I deal with his lies? Do I require verification and how will I get it? I ask to see phone bills to check for Allison's number. Dave flatly refuses. Mary, unfazed, forges on. She encourages us to devise a plan to divide our time with the kids. Make a schedule, she says, and what about the upcoming holidays?

"I like the idea of bird-nesting," Dave says. This involves keeping the kids in the marital house full time while the parents rotate in and out. We have friends, recently separated, who are doing it, and while it may work for them, it hardly seems feasible for us. It would require that we each have our own apartments, in addition to the house, and that we alternately use the same bedroom while we are in the house.

"We can't afford that."

"We can share an apartment," he says.

I know I've never been through this before, and I may be a bad judge of divorce protocol, but this seems asinine. I leave feeling overwhelmed, anxious, and more than a little afraid for my sanity.

I drive straight from dropping Jed at school to my friend Cathy's house to tell her the news. Cathy has a real estate agent coming to give an estimate on her house, but she tells me to stay. She makes me tea, and I ask if I can have a piece of toast. I don't remember when I last ate. As we talk, outrage begins rising in me. It feels like a catalyst of some kind, but I'm afraid of it and just so tired. The agent arrives, and he's trim and handsome and has the most beautiful, sonorous voice. While she gives him a tour, I lie on the sofa in her living room. It's soft and comfortable. I don't want to move. It soothes me to listen to the two of them talking in some distant room, to hear such innocuous words like *square footage, custom blinds, open floor plan*. I drift asleep but eventually start awake as they come into the living room.

"Don't worry," I tell him. "The crazy lady on the sofa doesn't come with the house. Woman having breakdown, not good for equity." I say it with no embarrassment. That's how happy I am for this respite.

From Cathy's I go to Target and buy Christmas stockings, robes, and toothbrushes for the kids. It's a start. Checking out, I overhear a young girl on her cell phone saying, "That's a boring idea for a gift. I only buy gifts that will benefit me." When I get home I go to the computer and order myself a pink iPod, with a leather case and an inscription: I AM HERE.

Merry Christmas to me.

It's late on a Tuesday night. The temperature outside has dropped to the single digits. I'm listening to the furnace run continuously, the heat seeping wastefully through the cracks of our decaying Victorian house. Dave sits across from me. It's my turn to say what I'm grateful for, and I don't want to. Dave waits. Finally I say, "I appreciate the courage it must have taken for you to tell me." I don't mean a word of this, but it seems to melt something in him and he says, tearfully, that I don't know how much that means to him. I move to put my arms around him, but he stops me.

"I don't want you to go there," he says. "I don't want this to turn the corner into something else."

I freeze, confused and angry. How am I ever going to find two grateful things to say about him every day? I may have to find one thing and repeat it. *I'm thankful you used a condom.* How's that?

While Dave is at work, Abigail and I take his clothes from the bedroom and hang them in a closet in the family room. She puts a vase of flowers and some framed photos of my kids on my bedside table.

"Is this happening?" I ask her. "Am I getting divorced?" I can barely say the word without a lump of fear threatening to gag me.

"Right now you're giving yourself space," she says. "That's all."

When Dave gets home, I say, "The bedroom is off-limits to you now. I moved you into the basement." He doesn't argue and I'm relieved. My next challenge is to explain it to the kids. Mary has prepared us: *If the children are needy, meet their needs. If they have questions, give simple, honest answers. Tell them Dad is sleeping on the sofa because Mom and Dad aren't getting along very well right now. You want everyone to be as happy as possible, so right now you're sleeping apart.* So I say this as casually as I can to the kids and it works.

That night, my first alone in our bedroom, I fall asleep a little easier and wake to the sound of a bird singing. The sky is black. It's not the first time I've heard birds singing in the night, and this doesn't seem natural. I wonder if it's unique to city birds. Maybe the city lights have them confused. Maybe they are as confused as I am, not knowing up from down or night from day. I hear Paul McCartney: *Blackbird singing in the dead of night. Take these broken wings and learn to fly.* I feel God very close to me, like a baby's breath on my cheek. He's nudged these words into my theta waves, and I will take them gently and hold them while they heal me. Like it or not, it's true: I have been waiting for this moment to arise.

4 No Drink for Me

By the end of the week, I have a bad cold that seems to be a result of so much crying. My nose is stuffy and my throat hurts. I'm sleeping enough, thanks to the hydroxyzine from Abigail, and though I'm foggy, I feel as if I'm able to lift my head and my gaze slightly higher and see, if not a path before me, at least some pebbles. My condition is a blessing, really, because I can tell the kids that Mommy is sick. Their exquisite perception has had them up between five and six the last two mornings, pushing into my bed.

As luck would have it, an annual girls' weekend was already planned for the weekend. There are six or seven of us who go to Michigan each year, most from Chicago, plus a couple of friends I've known for twenty or more years. Abigail is there. Also, my oldest friend, Carly. We go back to infancy. Our parents were friends, and she used to chase my brother Bryan around our church basement trying to kiss him.

Our destination is the Lakeside Inn, less than ninety minutes from Chicago, on the shores of Lake Michigan. It's a landmark inn, with a history as a resort and health spa in the late 1880s, then a longtime artist colony. Today it's a rustic, no-frills getaway decorated with the owner's collection of Native American artifacts. There are large, somber, black-and-white portraits in every room, photos so intense that Carly has to take the one of the wizened Indian matriarch off the wall and hide it before she can sleep. Dave and I were married here twelve years ago on a rainy and unseasonably cold September day. The theme of the weekend was "story." The invitations looked like bookmarks, the floral centerpieces were arranged atop piles of worn and weathered hardcover books, and the ceremony was performed by my long-time writing instructor, John, whom we called our narrator; he used the lyrics of the song *Paper Moon* to talk about how love makes us real to one another: *It's only a paper moon . . . but it wouldn't be make believe if you believed in me.* I wonder briefly if it's a good idea for me to be here, if it will be too painful, but I quickly dismiss this fear. Despite our wedding, I have a proprietary attitude toward the Lakeside Inn. I discovered it, and I've been meeting my girlfriends here for years.

We arrive amid a swirling snowstorm. The hundred-foot-long front porch and wooden rocking chairs are blanketed with snow, and there's more falling. The lobby is decked out for Christmas, and this startles me momentarily. *Christmas.* It's less than three weeks away. I avoid the thought, fearing that this respite, with its warm, pine-scented walls, twinkling lights, and blazing fire, may be the only serving of holiday cheer I'll get this year. I doubt I'll have the strength to decorate my own house. I can't even imagine shopping any more for my kids. An avalanche of feeling threatens at the pairing of those two thoughts—kids and Christmas—but I remind myself that the only pressing storm is outside. I am safe and, finally, warm as I hunker down in front of the massive fieldstone hearth.

I've lost my voice from the telling and retelling, and now, when I open my mouth, nothing comes out. I can only listen as my friends express their shock and surprise. They're especially intrigued by the fact that Dave poured himself a drink. *He didn't offer you one?* they ask, incredulous, and I shake my head. No drink for me. We have to laugh, and this becomes our first joke. That's movement, I think, when tragedy shifts to allow jokes. As I sit wrapped in my blanket, the fire dancing on my face, I feel like a tragic figure, someone from a bygone era, pale and bereft and therefore lovely, and this recasting of myself helps shift my story as well.

Romantic figures were never so sweaty, though. These last few days I've started sweating profusely, as if my body wants to remind me that I'm over forty and my chances of attracting a man ever again in my lifetime are quickly disappearing. The fact that dating even crosses my mind astounds me, but in the company of girlfriends it's inevitable. As women, we carry all stages of our lives with us, our Child, Maiden, Mother, and Crone, and this makes us more than a group of girls. We're a tribe. Femaleness is heightened when we gather, and no matter the various life roles we're currently playing, the maiden in each steps forward. Her dress is made of enchantment, expansion, enthusiasm, and new beginnings. The true beauty of women is our ability to see the maiden in each other.

But it's my inner crone who wins the day. She is repose, death, and endings. She's an old woman chilled to the bone, and she wants a comfy cardigan, dammit. So when we make our annual pilgrimage to the Lighthouse Place Outlet Mall, my girlfriends buy leather boots, Coach bags, sweet, colorful Hannah Anderson dresses for their girls, and other adornments, and I set out to construct a cocoon. I buy:

- an Eddie Bauer winter coat

- new gloves

- two pairs of thermal underwear

- hand warmers and toe warmers

- yoga pants and top

- an insulated travel coffee cup

- three pairs of wool socks

That night we have dinner and margaritas at a Mexican restaurant. Yes, a drink for me! I charge the entire bill. *It's on Dave,* I say, and we all cheer. I bask in our camaraderie, in the "life-sucks-sometimes-but-we're-all-in-it-together" feeling.

But back at the inn, in the room I'm sharing with Carly, the togetherness falls away and I'm back to feeling raw and alone. I'm nothing but a mother. Soon to be a *single* mother. When one of my children wakes sick in the night and needs the emergency room, my girlfriends will be asleep in their beds with husbands or lovers or, at least, hopes intact. When my kids misbehave, my thermal underwear will not help me make pivotal decisions. No yoga class will twist me into father, provider, disciplinarian, playmate, and every other parental facet they'll need. Face it, there is no village. There are high-rises and fences and locked doors. I can throw a rock from my front porch through my neighbor's window, and I won't know what to call her when she comes out screaming. Girlfriends may be a phone call away, but even the strongest voice on the end of a line can't do any heavy lifting.

For once, I try to cry, thinking it may help, but I'm too congested, too numb. I skip my sleeping pill and instead take Nyquil and two valerian capsules and lie down. Carly rubs my back and plays me a song by the band MercyMe on her iPod: *No matter what it is you're going through, even if you think you're far beyond where hope can see, I know there's a hand that's reaching out for you because He did the same for me.*

Carly was pregnant when we were seventeen. I remember the day she called me. I was in the tiny apartment where I lived with my mom and my sister a year after my parents' divorce. I was standing in the kitchen looking at a cute phone directory Carly had made out of a wooden shutter. She'd painted it, and when you flipped up the shutter, there were labels underneath for writing in names, numbers, and addresses. She was always clever that way, and the last I knew, she'd wanted to be a graphic designer.

Now she would be a mother. I was still very much a teenager, and had no idea what to say. We'd been friends since birth, but we didn't live in the same city anymore. I was set on college and hadn't kept in touch with her very well. I remember feeling sad and ashamed that something so important could happen to her without me.

Lying together at the Lakeside Inn, Carly and I are children again. I get a glimpse of someone I was before Dave, and know that I'll be someone again, without Dave. This is Grace. And this is Carly talking, telling me the things I missed: how she felt about being pregnant, how the boy's mother accused her of letting it happen and said hateful things to her, how she felt so alone. She tells me that she learned to see God as a seat belt holding her tight.

"I can take all the ups and downs of life now," she says. "I've got my seatbelt on and I'm ready for what comes."

We have no more words. The hissing radiator, the song on the iPod, it all falls away. I see a piece of Carly's heart that I've never seen and it's the most exquisite gift. I want to put it on a chain and wear it around my neck. I want to stay right here, in this silent sea, my oldest friend's hand on my back. I never knew a back rub could be so reverent and charged with compassion. I didn't know that the presence of a friend could feel like a parachute breaking a fall. Carly is a cool pillow to my fevered cheek.

Two thoughts come: I will live. And there is at least one person in the world I will let touch me when I'm cracked open.

5 Tapping a Geyser

Monday morning, Dave is in the bathroom when I hear his cell phone beep in the dining room. I go to the table and look at the screen: Ken. That means *Allison*. Before stopping to consider what I'm doing, I grab the phone and run into the front office, locking the door behind me. It's simple enough to display her incoming message: *You didn't answer my question. Welcome to reality.* The familiarity of her words baffles me. This is what rapturous, swept-off-your-feet, leave-your-family love looks like? It has the tone of a bicker between two long-married people. I can bicker with Dave this way, if that's what he wants. I hit the reply button but Dave has realized that I have his phone. He's at the door, pounding and telling me to open up. I step into the closet and begin punching at the letters. My hand is shaking so hard I fumble the words and have to figure out how to back up. Dave is yelling my name now. I nearly drop the phone but finally manage to type my response: *This is Dave's wife. R U or R U not going to leave my husband alone? Should I send you a pic of our kids?* There is no emoticon for what I'm feeling, so I leave it at that and hit send. I remain in the closet, waiting until my heart stops racing and Dave gives up and walks away. I know Dave can't leave for work without his phone, so I try calming myself before opening the door. One look at him, though, and venom rises in me. I practically hurl the phone at him.

"Be a man," I snarl. "Pick her or me and stop jerking me around!"

This time when Dave walks out the door, all I feel is relief.

I make an appointment to see Mary alone. Maybe I'm hoping that when Dave and I come back for a couple's session, Mary will be a little more on my side. I understand that she has to be neutral when we're both there, and of course I have Walter for my own therapy, but still, it's important to me to make sure she *understands*. I realize there is something controlling and immature about this, sort of like elementary school kids bribing the new girl to like them first. I don't care. Dave has established the "every man for himself" rule. I'm simply following.

I tell her about the ultimatum I gave Dave, and she tells me that I shouldn't say what I don't mean. She explains that in these situations, when "they"—*they?* My God! He's part of a group. A philanderers' group! Like the Shriners or Freemasons—when *they* are made to choose, they choose the other woman because that's where they feel loved. She adds that the three-week relationship Dave claims with Allison doesn't make sense. It sounds like Allison is pressuring him too, so as a result, Dave doesn't feel safe telling the truth because, even though I say I can take it, I react.

I stare at Mary a moment, wondering if I heard correctly. *Dave* doesn't feel safe?

"But I'm reacting to the fact that he's lying."

"In other words," she says, "you were prepared to not react to the truth, but not prepared for another lie."

"Exactly!"

"Then you have to be careful to say what you mean. He has to feel safe in order to tell the truth, and you have to determine how you'll deal with lies and verification. You'll need verifiable facts in order to rebuild trust."

"How on earth do I get those?"

She suggests phrases to use with Dave when I talk to him: *I'm curious about. . . What would that look like to you, Dave? Can you tell me . . . ? I want to understand . . .* I'm being spoon-fed language designed to coax Dave into communicating, and it makes me sick. I leave frustrated and hating this sense that I have to tiptoe around him, like he's suffering from something.

Although maybe he is. Abigail sends me a link to a site called Marriage Builders. Here I get another language lesson, this time in acronyms. I quickly learn that WS stands for Wandering Spouse. How delicately mealy-mouthed! It sounds like some poor gentle soul with Alzheimer's. But wait. The WS is also described as an alien. The site warns that there is no rationality. Would it have killed Mary to tell me that?

Abigail also sends me information on men suffering a midlife crisis, and I pounce on this wholeheartedly. I read that one stage is called Replay, where an otherwise stable man will act crazy and start an affair. He will become the total opposite of who he was before, doing things his wife never thought he'd do. He will feel entitled to take what he wants, regardless of who he hurts. Okay. Now I'm getting somewhere.

When I share this theory with my therapist, Walter, he quietly reminds me that Dave had his first affair ten years ago. Oh. *Right.*

"Don't rush to label him," he says. "Once you attach a label, you risk closing yourself off to what's really happening."

"Which is what?"

"The things he's told you, for starters. And probably things he hasn't."

Walter at least makes no excuses for Dave. In fact, I get the impression, though unspoken, that Walter is disgusted with Dave. This should make me feel better. It does. And then it doesn't.

Dave and I fall into our nightly routine with the kids, helping them with their homework, supervising piano lessons, making dinner. We're both hyper-attentive to them. Maybe that's why when Dave suggests that we all go to a movie, I agree. At least I can hide in a darkened theater. But once we're there, watching *Madagascar II*, I see there is no hiding. I feel myself slipping. I hunch down into my coat and hold my scarf in such a way that I can wipe my tears before the kids can see.

Later, when the kids are in bed, Dave sits at his computer in the dining room.

"Have you looked up divorce rules on the internet like Mary suggested?" I ask. I'm on the sofa eating plain yogurt. I feel shaky and weak, having had nothing all day but a little popcorn and Sprite at the movie.

"I started to, but haven't gotten far," he says. "Was there a specific website? I'm not finding anything."

I don't answer. My own research into surviving an affair advises cutting off emotional support. Basically, I need to resign all wife duties.

"Do you remember what she said?" he continues. "Because there's a ton of stuff coming up and it all seems vague." And on and on he goes, questioning me until I snap.

"Dave, I just Googled Illinois divorce rules! It's not that hard!"

Forget wife, I'm meant to be his secretary, even now. I should type a report entitled: *How to Divorce Me without Lifting a Fucking Finger.* I stand and walk toward him.

"Is she pregnant?"

He looks thoughtful, as if considering. "Not that I know of."

"Does she have kids?"

"No."

"How old is she?"

"I don't know."

I stare at him. "Our age? Younger? Childbearing years?"

"I don't know, and I'm not going to talk about it."

A curtain has come down somewhere inside Dave. Or maybe a steel wall. It's there when he answers me. It's in the mask of his face, the blankness of his gaze. For the first time I have trouble looking at him. A desperation fills me, and I want to take back the ultimatum I issued. I know who he's chosen, and it's not me.

I stand there helplessly before leaving the room. In the kitchen I putter about, feeling a simmering burn that will soon become familiar and frightening. I go back in and sit across from him.

"The night you told me, how did you think I would react?"

"About the way you did."

"But you must have known there was a chance I would ask you to leave. What would you have done?"

"I suppose I could have left for a day or two and given the kids a reasonable excuse."

"What if I had kicked you out indefinitely? What would you have told the kids then?" A new horror is dawning over me. Dave was willing to put the kids on the line, to roll the dice with their lives. Either that or he never believed I would do anything that wasn't orchestrated by him. I feel a rubber band tightening under my ribs. I am seeing Dave more clearly, but I'm seeing myself too. How well he's trained me. He serves me crumbs, and I mistake them for a feast.

I escape to the bedroom, climb into bed, and close my eyes. What comes to me is the face of my kids' babysitter. As we talked one day, she mentioned that she'd never known her father. She said she was walking in her small town with her mother when her mother pointed to a stranger across the street and said, "That's your father."

"Did he know you?" I asked. "Did he speak to you?"

Her face didn't change, but a tear sprang from one eye with such force it surprised us both. She faltered and shook her head, deeply embarrassed. I will never forget that moment and the sight of that lone tear. I had glimpsed the existence of a well that holds a pain so deep that to tap it is like tapping a geyser. This is our attachment to our parents, and it's primordial. It springs eternally, despite willful snubs or careless shrugs.

I lay with my fists clenched until I feel the rubber band stretch and break, snapped by a surge of something much stronger than anxiety: *hatred.*

6 Does Your Mother Know?

My parents have been divorced for twenty-seven years, but my mother does not speak favorably of my father, if she speaks of him at all. When I call her with the news, my face is burning; I'm embarrassed and ashamed that Dave is so like my father, who had his own string of affairs. I dread the inevitable comparison, and hate that my experience might invite more dad-bashing. Instead, my mother cries and says, "My heart breaks thinking of all the issues for the kids, things Dave can't begin to understand!"

Like me, she can't believe that this is the same man who made a toast only a week earlier to his "beautiful wife." We cry together, and I'm soothed, because there is nothing in the world like crying to your mother. I believe it waters some dry patch in us that, as adults, we tend to overlook, intent instead on staking up our blooming Proven-Winner lives.

And just as children and mothers are hard-wired with wisdom, wisdom itself is hard-wired to push through our emotional concrete to show its face. I see this when Logan brings me a book of Bible lessons my mother gave him and asks, "What's Isaiah 41 say?" I have to search to find a Bible that Carly gave me years earlier; I've looked at it maybe a handful of times. I show Logan how to find the verse. When he's finished, he leaves it open on the dining room table. The next morning, my aunt calls. She's heard the news from my mother.

"I want you to read something," she says. "This is from Isaiah 41. *Fear not, for I am with you. Be not dismayed, for I am your God. I will strengthen you, I will help you, I will uphold you with my righteous right hand.*"

I listen, awash in a sensation that's both stillness and electric charge.

"It's open right now in front of me."

This is my first brush with what I call Amazing Grace, though I'm not a newcomer to the pursuit of grace. I chose Grace as my daughter's middle name, blessing her with the belief that placing certain lines and curves on her birth certificate could catapult her to a higher plane. Consider these definitions of such a simple word: Seemingly effortless beauty; a temporary immunity, a reprieve; divine love freely given; the state of being protected; power granted by God.

Suddenly this whole derailment is taking on a certain tone. In the words of the poet Amy Lowell, it's striking a chord I knew existed, but seldom heard. And of course I hadn't heard, living as I was with my head in the sand. The ostrich pose may not be taught in any yoga class, but it has worked to keep away feelings that are not new to me. I've had a lifelong struggle with loneliness—no, something deeper than that—a fear of being disregarded, overlooked, cast off. It's a deep soul loneliness that can be kept at bay by a healthy social life or solid group of friends, but is finally revealed in long-term relationships, in the certainty that once someone really knows me, say for a decade or two, the truth will come out and I'll be found to be lacking.

I grew up believing I was "too sensitive" and "too quiet." I'd watch other people falling naturally into casual, lighthearted relationships and wonder how it came so easily. Maybe it was because I moved a lot as a kid and was so often in that social waiting room under the sign "new kid." Maybe it was from seeing my grandmother live alone for thirty years, then my mother. I didn't want to end up alone. I *wouldn't*, so help me God.

But God's help has come in the form of a big old belly laugh. It's like I've unrolled a giant fortune cookie message from the universe: Fear it and it will come. I'm stunned at the audacity of this smackdown. Perhaps it's this that makes me want to pay attention and convinces me that what is happening to me is more than a random act.

Still, grace can't protect me from the fact that Christmas is fast approaching; the inevitable pain of this looms over me like a guillotine. We always visit Dave's parents, who shower the kids with excess. There's been no talk of what will happen this year. It's up to me, I suppose, to stop thinking like a wife and find a new way to be. So I go to Abigail's house and drink tea and attempt to determine what I need. The effort of this makes me ache the way underused muscles ache after a workout, but finally the answer comes: I need my mother. She'll be in Nashville the week after Christmas so I use Abigail's computer to buy plane tickets for me and the kids to visit her there. The cost is $930, more than I've ever spent without Dave.

At home, the kids are fighting but Dave is in super-dad mode. He's strung Christmas lights, put plastic over the kids' bedroom windows, folded the laundry, and washed the dishes.

I calmly tell him that the kids and I will be going away during break.

"But you're going to my parents' too, right?"

"No."

"Why not?"

The teletext I deliver with my stare says, *figure it out, you dumb fuck!* I turn on my heels and leave.

Dave doesn't seem to get that his wife has resigned. To make it clearer, I begin shrugging whenever he asks one of his unending questions about how to do this or that. I wonder when I should make Dave move out. Despite my anger and discomfort having him around, terror still strikes me at the thought of living in the house alone. I see myself like some weak, newborn animal, a calf or lamb maybe, and I'm ashamed. Am I really so pathetic, so dependent? Why can't I summon the fury to act like a scorned woman? I could shred his clothes and throw them on the front lawn, maybe start sucking down a bottle of vodka and screaming obscenities. I picture Elizabeth Taylor in *Who's Afraid of Virginia Woolf?* She and Richard Burton could afford to destroy each other; their only child was likely a figment of their imaginations. I have three flesh and blood kids to protect. Still, wouldn't it be satisfying to make Dave fear *me*?

If I can't manage to throw his clothes on the lawn, at least I can find other things to throw out. I gather all the trinkets he's brought me from his business trips. He's been to Africa, India, France, the Netherlands, and Romania in the last few years. There's a scarf, a wooden elephant, white cotton sheets, a handcrafted metal hippo for the yard, jewelry. I dump it all on the table.

"I want you to keep those!" Dave protests when he comes home and sees the pile. "Nothing happened on my trips to Africa or India."

"What about Romania?"

He drops his gaze and admits to using a hooker in Romania. And, of course, Amsterdam.

"Get them out of here."

"I don't like to see you torturing yourself," he says. "Why are you imagining all those scenarios when everything I've told you is true?"

I notice his words. He's not saying that he's told me the truth, but that everything *he's told me* is true. Dave is an ad man, a wordsmith, and though I have certainly been clueless, I'm not stupid. Words are my strong suit as well, and I vow to listen carefully to every syllable Dave utters from now on.

"I'm not sneaking off to places, seeing her."

"I wish I could believe you, but put yourself in my place."

I hate that I'm asking this. It's painfully clear that Dave has no ability or desire to put himself in my place, and hoping otherwise keeps me playing the fool. But I want . . . I want . . . to go *back*, I guess, to somehow make this right. I sit up and reach for his hand, a gesture that brings me to tears.

"What I said to you the other day about picking her or me was in anger. I didn't mean it. I don't want a divorce." Remembering Mary's advice, I add, "I don't need a response from you."

I get none. Dave leaves, and I lie down, hoping to sleep. But I'm not alone in the room. Terror is sneaking in, gathering like wisps of black smoke in the corners, curling up the walls, until it comes together in a mass above my bed. It blots out all light and sound as it sits on my chest. I ask it to dismantle me quickly. Take me apart, leave what you want, I don't care. I begin to shake violently. I must *do* something. But the black smoke is in my head too, and I can't think. Before I realize it, I'm up and running to Dave. He's stretched out on the sofa watching a baseball game.

"I'm having a panic attack. Can you please come lie with me?"

He follows me into the bedroom, gets on the bed behind me, and puts an arm over my stomach. The sound of my teeth chattering is the loudest sound in the room. After a while he says, "Everything is going to be okay." He says a friend told him that people come through these things better than ever.

"I still see us doing things as a family," he says. "This won't destroy us."

Now I want him to shut up. I don't understand a thing he says. I *am* destroyed, and I am part of *us*. I hope he never uses that word again. It obviously has no meaning for him anymore, if it ever did.

Our daughter April's fourth birthday is two days before Christmas, and though I've resigned wife duties, I don't intend to resign Mom duties. Unfortunately, I can't seem to muster the strength or enthusiasm to throw her a party. Dave offers to do it, and I'm relieved but also annoyed because his exuberance seems clownish and forced. I also feel a nasty smugness, as if once he has to deal with the realities of parenthood—party planning, meal planning, housework, being a taxi driver—without my help, he'll certainly come to his senses and say, *oh, never mind that divorce business, I can't handle this!*

It's the opposite. Dave puts together a seventies dance party. He moves the table out of the dining room, hangs streamers from the chandelier, and inflates several dozen balloons. I don't lift a finger except to make a pot of coffee and wipe urine off the toilet seat. I stay in the kitchen mostly, and the mood there is subdued and awkward, since the handful of other moms around me all know that Dave "is leaving." What an odd concept, considering he is firmly installed on the dance floor, playing *Dancing Queen* with the girls. Actually, ABBA is blaring from the stereo, a song called *Does Your Mother Know?* I don't witness the opening of gifts or any of the games Dave leads them through. I don't notice what April is wearing, or how she's interacting with her friends. I feel as if I'm in a fog, conscious only of my own acute embarrassment and desire to disappear.

Afterward I lie in bed and cry, getting up late in the afternoon to take the kids caroling with a group of neighbors. A few hours later I take a sleeping pill and fall into a fitful sleep until 1:30 a.m., when something wakes me. Dave is in my room. He's returned from being out with a friend. He wants to hold me.

I say nothing as he climbs in bed and puts his arm around me. I should be memorizing the feel of him against me. It will likely never happen again. But all I can think about is the way the house looked, decorated for the party. Dave made a real effort. And how difficult it must have been for him, alone on the dance floor with the kids, the adults gossiping in the kitchen, judging him. I feel sorrow for him and it rumbles in me like an approaching avalanche, threatening to take me down. "There is nothing heavier than compassion," writes Milan Kundera in *The Unbearable Lightness of Being*. So I run from it before it can crush me, leaping, latching onto the only branches I can reach—the hard facts of what Dave has done, the shape of a woman's face, the lines of entangled limbs, a different bed, *several* beds, how many? I clutch at these sharp things to keep from being buried alive.

7 Let It Snow

On Christmas Eve I have an appointment with Walter, and we work to counteract my dread of the holiday with the affirmation, "I am strong." He uses muscle testing to help me feel the energy that these words bring to my body. First I hold one arm out straight and try to resist while he pushes down. My arm sinks weakly. I do it again after repeating the affirmation and my arm stays firm. He reminds me that this energy is available to me at all times, and I believe him.

But my strength is short-lived. I'm invited to a birthday brunch, so I take the kids while Dave goes shopping on his own. Bruce and Kathleen are old friends with two boys roughly the same age as Jed and April. Bruce celebrates his birthday like this every year, with a small group of friends, and though we haven't come before, he was kind enough to invite me this year. Kathleen is Bruce's second wife, making him one of the few friends I have who has been divorced. I cringe at this unwanted bond, but if it means being included in today's festivities, I'll take it.

We arrive early, before anyone else. Their house is lovely, with a crackling fire in the family room, the gorgeous aroma of coffee, bacon, and baked french toast floating from the kitchen, and two friendly dogs to pet, but I feel lost and disoriented and only want to lie down. Kathleen shows me to their guest room and tells me I can use it as long as I need. So while the kids play in the basement, I curl up on the bed and try to hold myself together. The terror returns. *No, no, please not now.* It cracks open the door and sidles inside. It's been stalking me, and now I have nowhere to hide. I look around the comfortable room and repeat, *I am strong, I am safe*, but I keep thinking of the way Dave comes into my room whenever he wants, even in the middle of the night. I tell myself that he only wants to talk or to hold me. Still, I don't like it.

How is it possible to be afraid of a person I've known for twenty years?

Maybe it's the holiday, maybe it's the haunting nature of this question, but I start thinking of my sister Melanie, who is nine years younger. More than fifteen years earlier, when she was sixteen years old, she attempted suicide. She took every pill she could find, including a bottle of our mother's blood pressure medication. A teenage friend happened to call and, alarmed by Melanie's slurred speech, alerted his father, who is a psychiatrist. My mother was awakened by them pounding on the front door.

I was at work when I got the news. I'd just started as a waitress at the Chicago Diner, a popular vegetarian restaurant on Halsted Street, in a neighborhood known as Boystown. I didn't know my co-workers yet, but they all seemed progressive and aloof, and I hoped my own hipness would increase in this new environment. After someone handed me the phone and I listened to Dave describe an impossible scenario of pills, an ambulance, and stomach pumping, I became excessively apologetic to the server, to the busboy, to the owner. "I may be able to come back later," I babbled, before rushing out the door. I had an inexplicable urge to let them know that this wasn't the *real* me. *I'm not a crazy unreliable woman with a busload of baggage. I'm a good worker. You'll like me.*

Rushing back to Ohio to visit Melanie after she was released from the psychiatric ward was like gearing up to box the darkness. I had no idea what to say. I flailed helplessly when faced with her pain. It was like a chasm that, to me, appeared overnight, yet how often does the earth move that way? No. Loved ones become strangers drip by drip, teardrop by teardrop. How did I let it happen? Then *and* now? And what other catastrophes are on the horizon that I'm failing to see? How can my children be safe when their mother is locked in a bedroom not knowing how she'll make it through the day?

But I would *never* do what she did. I'm not crazy—a word defined by Webster as full of cracks and flaws. Also erratic and out of the ordinary. One sounds inevitable and human, the other frightening. Which am I? Normal crazy, or crazy crazy? *Walter, I need you!* I try to breathe and repeat *I am safe. I am strong.* It's Christmas, 2008. I may be in an unfamiliar room, but it's a quiet room, on a quiet street, in Chicago's Ravenswood Manor neighborhood. *Safe.* Just around the corner is Governor Rod Blagojevich's house. A few weeks ago, when federal agents arrested him on federal corruption charges for trying to sell an Illinois senate seat, Blagojevich put on a jogging suit and did jumping jacks in front of them, then laid on the floor of his living room. *Erratic.* He was released on $4,500 bail; he's likely home now, two streets away, celebrating the holiday with his family, a Secret Service sedan parked out front. *Normal.* My name is Tammy, and I'm getting divorced and becoming a single mother of three. O*rdinary.*

I have that sense again that I've done something terribly wrong. I'm losing someone I love, and there's nothing I can do about it. The pull of the past is too strong, and I let it have me. I hear Dave singing the song he wrote for my sister after she was released from the hospital. It was simple and sad and perfect, and why did he have to do such a lovely thing? He played it on an acoustic guitar while sitting on my mother's bed, my sister huddled nearby in her black, baggy clothes—black, black, everything she wore was black. I couldn't hide my tears as Dave began to sing:

*Your sister and I, we think about you every time we walk
past the skate shop on Halsted Street and Altgeld Avenue. And
we yin and yang about you every time we see that fat plastic
Buddha in the drugstore window calling out your name.*

And oh, Melanie, she says, I'll never have your perfect skin.

And oh, Melanie, she says, I'll never have your pretty hair.

*And oh Melanie, she cries, I never seem to have enough
time with you.*

*Everybody's room looks a little black in the dead of the
night. But open up your door a crack, and we'll do our best to
cast you a little more light.*

Fifteen years have passed, but I can't hear or think of this song
without crying. Each time I've cried, it felt cleansing, with a little
more of the hurt washing away, the chasm filling, as it will over time,
with soothing water. There was enough relief to float me through
an intervention, because Melanie became addicted to drugs, beginning with marijuana before dissolving in the poison of crystal
methamphetamine. By the time we realized how far she'd fallen, she
was living in Colorado. She'd been married and divorced, and the
rare times we heard from her, we were barraged with stories of her
estranged husband's craziness, his drinking, parties, and violence.
Conversations with her were emotional and rambling, but we put
this down to stress. We thought she might be bipolar. It wasn't until a
call came from the Colorado Family Services Unit in early 2007 telling us that her six-year-old son had been taken from her and placed
with his father that we learned the truth. She and her husband had
dabbled in drugs together, but he was able to pull back and settle into
functioning alcoholism. She was not.

I spent hours on the phone to Colorado then, with neighbors,
detectives, and social services, piecing together a shocking picture:
my nephew locked out of the house after school, breaking a window

to get in, strangers coming and going at all hours, holes punched in walls and filled with rotting food, used needles on the floor, and finally, Melanie begging the neighbor to give her a urine sample for a drug test.

My mother, two brothers, and I turned to an intervention service in Indiana and were assigned to a facilitator named Ben, a fit, good-looking twenty-eight-year-old with a sand-colored crew cut. He was a former heroin, crack cocaine, and meth addict, and his stories horrified us. He told how he had been on a sofa, beyond caring, while a friend died on the floor beside him. How he rode his motorcycle 180 miles an hour down a highway near Las Vegas, certain he was being chased by aliens. As shocked as we were, Ben gave us hope. If he could come back from that hell, so could Melanie. First, we needed $6,000. Dave and I refinanced our house to get it, and the planning began. Our first assignment was the most difficult. We were each to write a letter to Melanie, sharing specific memories we had of her and telling her why we loved her, then explaining how her drug addiction was affecting us. The letter was to end with the sobering vow that if she did not go to rehab, we would not see or speak to her again.

It was a chilly Friday in late March when we arrived at an Embassy Suites hotel in Colorado Springs, Dave and my mother and I flying from Chicago, my brother Bryan from Louisiana, and my younger brother, Ray, from Iraq, where he was contracted as a security guard for a private military company. Even my father joined us, making a stressful event all the more volatile; it was the first time he and my mother would face each other since Melanie's suicide attempt years earlier.

Tragedy, always the equalizer, made our dramas disappear, as did the round table where we gathered to begin preparations. It smoothed the corners between us so that, facing one another, we were finally united in a common cause. Ben asked us to open the two-inch binders in front of us, and we began an education in drug addiction and intervention methods that would last all day. Before brainstorming various scenarios based on Melanie's possible condition, Ben told us to read our letters aloud to the group. He warned that this would be the hardest part, but that we needed to lessen the emotional charge surrounding it. When it was my turn, I found I couldn't speak. I felt my throat being squeezed by one hand, my heart by another. In a panic, I stood, then sat down, then stood again, wanting to run. Embarrassed by my display, I finally managed to read my words: *I love you, Melanie, but until you agree to get help, I will not see you or speak to you or respond to you in any way. This is goodbye.* And then I cried for the long blond hair I saw floating around Melanie's nine-year-old face as she hung from the monkey bars, for the long legs that splashed me in the pool the summer we decided she was part mermaid, for the memory of her visiting Chicago with her friend, the three of us sharing makeup in the bathroom, hearing Melanie whisper *my sister's cool, isn't she?* when I left the room. I cried it all out and saw my heartbreak reflected in the circle as each of us imagined the unimaginable.

And Ben was right. Once the letters were read, space was cleared for optimism and action. My mother would call Melanie and ask her to come to the hotel in the morning. She'd say she had come for Melanie's birthday, as a surprise, and that she had money for her. Be prepared to wait, Ben said, explaining that crystal meth destroys the brain's ability to track time.

"I'll be able to tell right away where her high is," he added. "Whether she just used or is coming down. Then we'll know how to play it. The paranoia will be our biggest challenge. If we can get her to stay past the first few minutes, we've got a chance."

That night my brothers, Dave, and I watched the crude mockumentary movie, *Borat,* with our dad in his hotel room and tried to laugh away our fears. Then came a sleepless night and a breakfast buffet that I barely touched. At last my mother's phone rang, and it was Melanie. She was on her way with Jerry, her current boyfriend and, according to the police, her drug dealer. Jerry had an arrest record for narcotics and domestic violence and was, the detective said, not someone to be messed with. Ben coached my mother on how to get rid of him, and we nervously joked that, if that didn't work, my younger brother Ray, a former Marine sniper who was always armed, would step in.

Thirty minutes went by, then an hour. Melanie called again, saying she would be there soon. Another hour went by. When she finally arrived, Jerry presented a different, unexpected challenge. He had his eighteen-month-old daughter with him. Ben quickly convinced Jerry to hand me the sleeping child and leave for a few hours. In those first hectic moments after Melanie stepped into the hotel room and saw us all there, while she was still smiling and believing that this was all an innocent birthday surprise, I settled the baby on the bed in the next room.

Melanie took a seat between my mother and older brother on the sofa, and I sat beside Dave, an uneasy smile plastered to my face while my mind screamed, *she's not running, she's not running!* I made myself look at her. Always a beauty, with long strawberry blonde hair, brown eyes, and a wide easy smile, she'd aged into someone I didn't recognize. I caught myself imagining that she was a stranger, that I was in this room observing a different family. My job was merely to record and report, a role I often took on in order to remove myself from an experience. I made mental notes: she was jittery and disoriented, her skin had a yellow cast, her teeth looked odd, as if too big for her mouth, and her hair, her lovely long hair, was brittle and dull.

Ben introduced himself as a friend who was there to help. He skillfully laid out the facts and how he was uniquely qualified to tell her where she was headed. Get treatment or die, he said. He turned to my mother and asked her to share what she'd written. His meaningful look signaled the importance of this moment. My mother took Melanie's hand and read her letter. She was tearful but surprisingly strong. I stared at the floor, trying to swallow past the lump in my throat, listening to the heartfelt memories, the pleas, the painful ultimatum. At times there were flickers of emotion from Melanie, glimpses of who she'd been, but then the imposter would return with the dull eyes and expressionless face. We each read our letters, my brother Ray going last, and when he was finished, he paused. With his next words, his face crumpled. After Bosnia, he said, he came horrifically close to climbing a tower with a rifle and taking people out.

"I nearly went postal. I seriously thought about it."

The room froze, more startled by this Marine's tears than if he'd fired his gun right then and there.

"I got help," he said, wiping his eyes. "You need to get help." No one moved. No one breathed. This man, who had jumped from airplanes, endured waterboarding, and taken the lives of men with single precision shots, had just done the bravest thing he would ever do.

The gift was lost on Melanie, and when I saw her unmoved, anger and disgust flared in my chest. I wanted this over. I wanted this shell of a person out of my sight.

Ben became very blunt as he laid out the deal. There was a flight booked that afternoon. She would go to Pasadena, California, where there was a bed reserved for her. Ben would accompany her to the center. She had to go immediately, without contacting anyone.

"But my dogs. . . ." she began. Melanie's son—my nephew—had been taken from her. She was about to see her parents, her entire family, for the last time, and she was worried about her dogs?

Melanie used the bathroom, her cell phone in her hand. She went out on the balcony and smoked a cigarette with my brother Bryan while my mother and I fussed over the baby, who was beginning to stir. Ben was optimistic. *She's coming down*, he said. She asked about the flight, about the length of the treatment. We unzipped the duffle bag we brought for her, with new T-shirts and sweatpants and pajamas. Even cigarettes. Plus a set of sheets I'd picked out at Target, lime green with pink flamingos and palm trees. See? We'd thought of everything!

It all happened fast after that. The baby was in Melanie's arms. She ran into the hall. Jerry was there, coming up the stairs. There was running, my mother chasing, reaching for her, shouting that reverberated in the hotel atrium. *Don't you touch me! I hate you!* Melanie and Jerry climbed into a beat-up Ford flatbed truck and were gone. We haven't heard from Melanie since.

Remember that, Dave? Remember how we went through that together? How we cried together?

Now Dave is lost to me too. And the pain of *him* is tied to the pain of *her*, and what was beautiful and pure is tarnished. Every one of Dave's kind acts, every extraordinary gesture of love is contaminated by his betrayal. All my memories are recast in a new light, and like precious photos left in the sun, they are distorted and fading. Who am I, now that my past is corrupted?

Out the window I see snow falling. I wonder if it's snowing in Colorado and if Melanie still lives there. If she lives. She may be dead. But wouldn't I know that? Wouldn't I feel it? I know nothing.

I'm still in the guest room when people begin arriving for Bruce's birthday brunch. I hear the stomp of snowy shoes and cheerful greetings muffled by hearty hugs. I'm shaking and, once again, I can't get enough air. I don't dare walk downstairs and disrupt the party but I need help. I manage to call Abigail on my cell phone. I ask her to dial Bruce's home phone to see if he can come upstairs—a ridiculous runaround, but it works. Moments later, I hear the phone ringing, then the sound of feet running up the stairs. Bruce opens the door. Just like that day in the Chicago Diner, I want to hide my face and tell him I'm not this person. Really I'm not.

"I'm so sorry," I say, gasping. "I don't mean to ruin your birthday. I'm so scared and I can't breathe."

He sits beside me on the bed and puts his arms around me.

"This will pass. I promise," he says. He covers me with blankets and holds my hand. We sit that way for awhile as the house fills with his friends. He offers to bring me a plate of food. I decline. I'm so grateful to him. I want to say it, but when I open my mouth, nothing comes out. Just like with Melanie, and with Dave. I don't have the right words. I am so . . . *lacking*, so ineffectual. So frightfully small.

8 Silent Night

It's 6:00 a.m. on Christmas morning, and Jed is the first one awake. I hear him squealing in the living room. He's seen the Playmobil ark that Dave set up late last night, and he's shouting for April to wake up. I drag myself out of bed to watch them open their gifts. Dave has gotten the boys iPods, and they love them. I take out the pink iPod I bought for myself and show it to them, saying it's from Santa. And then I'm done. I've been up only a half hour, but I go back to bed and sleep until noon. Even then I can't rouse myself. I call to Dave, asking him to come in. He sits on the bed and I take his hand. My tears have made my face a runny mess, and I need a Kleenex.

"How does one person do this to another?" I ask. "I gave you three children. I gave you the most precious gift in the world. Whatever you think of me, I gave you those kids. How could you treat me this way?"

He closes his eyes, rests his chin in his hand, and says nothing. I let go of his hand and roll over.

Soon Logan, Jed, and April come to kiss me goodbye. They're leaving for Dave's parents' house. When the front door closes the house grows very quiet and I wait, strangely detached, to see if this is it for me. Is this the bottom? Can this get worse, and what would that look like? As it turns out, the afternoon looks like an afternoon, neither blessed nor cursed. I drink some orange juice. I take a shower. I breathe a word of thanks that I have somewhere to go. The neighbors have invited me to dinner, so at 4:30 p. m. I walk down the block, my footsteps silent in the gentle snow. It's dark already and lights are glowing, strings of icicle lights that I used to think were the very glow of happiness. Now I assume nothing. Does this count as a Christmas gift?

My neighbors Jason and Ellen are one of the reasons Dave and I bought this house in Chicago's Albany Park neighborhood. Jason and Dave have been friends for years, both musicians who have collaborated on several projects. He and Ellen are a decade older than us and have lived on this block for more than fifteen years. Thanks to them, we enjoyed an instant sense of community from the moment we moved in. They have two teenagers, and the five of us share a feast of turkey, stuffing, sweet potatoes, Brussels sprouts, coleslaw, and pumpkin pie. I'm startled by how much I'm able to eat. The last time I remember enjoying food was at the Thanksgiving dinner Dave and I hosted for our friends, just a month ago. Is it a coincidence that it's the same menu? Perhaps nostalgia is cellular and lives in the lining of the stomach, trumping all else. Or perhaps the numbness and nausea of the last four weeks are behind me.

After dinner, their kids disappear upstairs and Ellen pours coffee as they wait for me to find the right words. They've heard the news, of course, but not the details, and express their shock when I tell them all of it. Has it occurred to me to stop sharing the story the way it was delivered to me, as a one-two-three punch? Affair. *Ker-pow!* Escorts. *Wham!* Las Vegas love. *Ouf!* Yes, I've considered skipping all that, but I need to keep speaking this trifecta to remind myself where I place in this horse race. It's only when I let all three things sink in that I know *all bets are off.* My marriage is over.

Jason is shaking his head, confused. "It seems like Dave has a serious problem. Like he doesn't know what he's doing."

"Jason and I were talking about the fight he was in, in Atlanta," Ellen says. I'd forgotten that a couple of months earlier Dave had returned from a business trip with a black eye from a bar fight. The story was striking mostly because it involved Dave, someone who, despite having three brothers, has never been a fighter.

Jason pushes his plate aside. "I said to Ellen, who does that? A forty-something married man with kids doesn't go around getting in fights. It seemed very odd to us."

"Do you think he's on drugs?" Ellen asks.

"I mean, my God, he could be charged with criminal endangerment for the prostitutes!" Jason interjects.

Their bluntness could easily throw me into a panic, but from them the questions feel reasonable and necessary. Jason and Ellen are one of the few married couples I know who seem to genuinely like each other. I've never heard one disparage the other, and that alone sets them apart. It makes me trust them in a way I'm realizing I can't trust just anyone. I've already experienced various reactions to my situation, from the lifelong pals who check in regularly, to those who say *let me know how I can help* but don't follow up, and even some who react as if I'm relaying a weather report. Abigail has told me not to be surprised by the unpredictable nature of friends' reactions, that the treatment I get is more a reflection of fears and beliefs that have nothing to do with me. *You never know what's really going on in other relationships,* she said. She also warned me that I don't want to forever be the friend in crisis and to prepare for the drama to wear off quickly. This makes me paranoid, wondering if it's a hint. Is she saying that she's tired of hearing it? I have to choose my confidantes carefully. I know that silence is golden, but commiseration is more precious to me right now.

"Have you been tested?" Ellen asks quietly.

The answer is no, not yet. But, of course, it's also yes. Tested beyond what I could have imagined, and the test continues with more difficult questions arising all the time. By the time I get home, five hours later, I have scored one decision: I need a lawyer.

The kids return from their grandparents laden with gifts. They rush to me, asking "Mama, do you feel better?" I smile and hug them and busy myself with packing for our trip. We're leaving the next day for Nashville. As I load the van with our suitcases, Dave stands on the porch, watching. He's on his cell phone and I hear him say *I'll see you soon.* Who is he talking to? What will he do while we're gone? Will he get on a plane to Vegas? The questions torture me, making a stressful flight with three young kids all the more trying. To amuse myself I fiddle with my cell phone and change the icon that was assigned to Dave's number. I delete his photo and choose a skull and crossbones instead.

When we land in Nashville, the sun is shining and the warmth is a tonic after the ice and snow of Chicago. I curl up in my mother's La-Z-Boy recliner next to the picture window and watch the birds gather at the feeder, wrens and red-headed woodpeckers and occasionally a cardinal, always my favorite. Before long, Dave calls. I see the skull and crossbones icon appear on my phone, so I hand it directly to Logan. I don't anticipate his eye for detail, and when he asks me why Daddy's picture is gone I have to think fast.

"I gave Daddy a pirate look," I say, and quickly add that there weren't many icons to choose from.

The kids each talk to him, and when April is done she holds the phone out to me. "You want to talk to him, Mom?"

I take it from her and flip it shut.

"Why didn't you say anything?" Jed asks.

"The battery was about to die," I fib.

"You could have talked until it went out," he says.

I duck my head, ashamed of my behavior. Where do I draw the line between being protective of myself and ridiculous and hurtful in front of the kids? I become more confused later when I read an email from Dave. *I'm still your old friend,* he writes. *I kept some things from you, but that doesn't change our friendship.*

I don't know how to respond to that, so I don't. This is an approach I don't think I've ever tried in my life, but I'm beginning to see the merit of it. Maybe it's easier, being with my mother. I can be the child, without responsibility, excluded from decision making and relieved of even the simplest day to day tasks. I sit by the window, eventually flipping through some of my mom's books. There's one on forgiveness. In it I find: *Now is the time to forgive this man and help him back on his feet. If all you do is pour on the guilt, you could very well drown him in it. My counsel now is to pour on the love. 2 Corinthians 2:7.*

God how I hate the F word! *Forgiveness.* I've tried practicing forgiveness in my relationship with my father, and I'm never sure what I'm supposed to feel. But *love,* I find that easier to contemplate.

When was the last time I told Dave I loved him? Did I say it enough? Why didn't I say it more? Why was I so stingy? Would it even have made a difference?

I read the quote again and pray: *God, show me how to pour on the love.*

Nothing. I don't feel it. I'm sorry, God, but I can't help Dave get back on his feet. I need to find my own. I begin by walking with the kids in the woods. We're excited to find a deer blind that they think is a fort made by a runaway slave, or a lost boy, or a wood fairy. Next we eat pizza. We watch Steve Martin in *The Jerk.* It's one of my mom's favorite movies, and we tell the kids they'll love it. We forget that it's rated R and I spend a ridiculous amount of time diving to cover little ears and eyes, which makes my mom and me laugh as if we're filming our own slapstick comedy.

I load my new iPod with some of my mom's albums: The

Commodores, Bette Midler, The Carpenters, Elvis Presley's *How Great Thou Art*—music from my childhood that gives me glimpses of this thing called ME who existed before Dave. Occasionally I stop what I'm doing, or not doing, and try on the thought: *I am divorced. I am a single mother.* I can't look at that picture without seeing a bigger, darker one, a foreboding storm cloud crackling with the thunderbolt *I am alone (unlovable/broken/defective).* I try to imagine what it will look like, this life with just me and my kids. I know the cliché—if I'm okay, they'll be okay. I feel okay right now, sitting in the sun, away from the trappings of my life, away from Dave. The kids seem more relaxed too. It can't be good for them to absorb the energy of betrayal, confusion, and anger that pervades our house. I resolve that any love I have I'll pour on them. But even this love feels depleted, reduced to a trickle where once a river raged. What if I'm forever in a dry spell? Will I remain brittle and dried up, and how then will I buoy my children?

This fear surges each night when I tackle the bedtime routine on my own. I'm quickly overwhelmed and impatient and hear myself snapping at the kids to hurry up and go to sleep, an oxymoron that makes me feel ignorant and nasty. I read somewhere that children lose both parents in a divorce—one is physically gone and the other is so changed by assuming both roles that he or she becomes unfamiliar. So as I help April brush her teeth, and promise to read to Jed, and remind Logan to turn off his iPod, I do my best to keep this stranger in me away from my kids. And when Jed throws his arms around me and says, "Mom, I'm glad that God made you because you're extra huggable and kissable," I'm so grateful to him for reminding me who I am.

The subject line of the email in front of me says *Friend Needs Divorce Attorney.* I'm scanning the list of names and numbers sent by my friend Karen when Logan comes up behind me. Before I can shut the screen he says, "Who needs a divorce lawyer?"

"No one you know," I mumble. "And please don't read my private emails."

I double my efforts to be cautious after that, but an attorney named Harry returns my call while I'm out in my mom's car with the kids. I pull into the parking lot of a hamburger stand, quickly order a bag of takeout food, then shove french fries at the kids through the car window while I talk and pace the parking lot.

Harry's questions are brisk: Where does Dave work and what is his position? How long have I been a stay-at-home mom? Do I know our income and expenses? My story is not the star here. This guy wants facts. My relief is immediate, until he starts to talk about dissipation. I don't know what this means. Is Dave squandering marital assets? he asks, reminding me that half of everything is mine. He suggests putting a freeze on Dave's IRA account and filing for immediate temporary support. All of this strikes me as drastic and premature. I haven't even filed for divorce. And shouldn't I interview several attorneys?

Harry solves this himself when he says, "I'm happy to give you this advice, and feel free to call me again if you need to, but I'm going to refer you to another attorney in my building. To be blunt, I'm a Lexus, and you need a Toyota."

I'm passed to Scott, an attorney in his mid-thirties with his own practice. He's friendly but brisk, sort of the happy bulldog type. I like his energy and decide this is a good time to trust that I'm being brought to the right person at the right time. We make an appointment for the following week, when I'm back in Chicago. I imagine our meeting will be a fact-finding mission, a dipping of my toe in the legal sea. I'm still not sure if I should file, or wait for Dave to do it. I don't know if Dave will have a change of heart, or even what the state of my heart is.

But two days later I get an email from Dave that's like a bucket of ice water over my head. He's closed our joint account. There's no explanation, just one sentence letting me know I'm cut off. I'm a thousand miles away with seventeen dollars in my purse and one useless bank card. I call Scott.

"Game on," he says. "He's obviously got an attorney." Scott instructs me to cease all contact with Dave except via email. "Be polite, direct, and keep all correspondence business-like. Discuss your relationship in a therapy setting only."

"But—"

"Trust me. You don't want your kids living in a war zone."

He tells me to request a copy of the bank account ledger and monthly budget from Dave, and to make a list of our assets. "In order to protect yourself financially, you'll need to file," he says.

"How do I pay you?" I ask.

"My retainer is five thousand dollars. I'll petition the court for Dave to cover that."

I hang up and stare at the phone in my hand. The receiver, attached by its curly cord to my mom's wall-mounted telephone, looks like a little barbell and as I slowly replace it, I get the sense I'm in training now. Training for estrangement. Bulking up and pulling in. Game on. Ready or not.

The game changes with another phone call later the same day, this one from my friend Carly. A growth has been detected in her uterus. She needs surgery. A hysterectomy is certain. Cancer is possible. In an instant, perspective is restored, and I am both blessedly free of Dave and desperately afraid for Carly. If someone told me two months ago to choose between two fateful events, that my husband would leave or that my best friend would have cancer, which would I choose? I wouldn't have been able to even entertain the idea of Dave leaving. Now my feeling is *let him go!* Losing Carly would be the real darkness.

In fact, as I sit here on this New Year's Day, anticipating the year ahead, I wonder at all the ways my life will change. To my surprise, it's becoming easier to imagine being without Dave, and I realize that this is because, in many ways, he has already been absent. I recall a recent moment when I was weeping on Abigail's sofa, listing all the things I would never be able to do on my own—the shopping and feeding and bedtimes and driving and homework—when she stopped me by saying, "You mean the things you already do?"

The icy feeling comes over me again. It's time for a wide-eyed look at what was really occurring in my life and what I wanted to see. For as long as I can remember, I've been programmed with a fear of being alone. When I was young, my family moved often, so being "the new girl" was a phase I endured the way others endured braces or a pimply forehead. I craved invisibility but was also crushed by it. I learned to be watchful and wary, adept at discerning the friendliness of the "normals" from the over-eager flattery of the social leeches. I came to appreciate being "chosen" and to believe that the only options were to be chosen or to be alone. My skill was in observing the social tides, knowing which current would move me forward, and which would sweep me out to sea to be forgotten. Having the power to make my own choices was never a consideration.

On the first day of my job as a copywriter, when Dave, a writer in my group, invited me for lunch, I fell gratefully into his sphere. His experiences overlapped with mine. Like me, he went to a Big Ten school. He was also a second child with three siblings, same as me. We'd both boldly struck out for the big city, leaving small towns behind. But he was larger than me too. He'd been at the job longer and was clearly treasured for his creativity. He played in a band, had a car, and a nice apartment. We quickly became friends, and then one night at Foster Beach, the waves of Lake Michigan breaking softly and inevitably in the dark, Dave expressed his desire that we date. I saw no reason to say no, so that left only yes. We kissed once, tentatively, and our couple-hood was set as surely as the giant rocks that lined the shore. A few days later, at Dave's apartment, I used the bathroom and saw a Post-it note lying in the garbage can. It was in Dave's hand-writing, addressed to his roommate Bob, and said *Tammy is mine!*

I belonged to someone. It was as if my life had been a carousel, round and round without landing anywhere, and here was Dave hold-ing a claim check, ready to haul me home and unpack me. I had arrived. The where didn't matter. What mattered was that I was no longer travel-ing alone.

Just before our flight home, I give in and call Dave, asking him to pick us up at the airport. I hate to ask him for anything, but I don't have money for a cab, and Abigail is not available. The ride home is awkward. I stare out the window while Dave cheerfully chats with the kids about their adventures in Tennessee. I have to be grateful for his ability to fake it for their sakes; I'm not able to do the same.

I dread being back in the house with him. We haven't devised a parenting schedule, and being together again is overly familiar and newly strange. Perhaps sensing this, the kids head for seclusion, the boys bolting downstairs to their toys and TV, April crawling under the dining room table. She has her Playmobil animals: an elephant, zebra, lion, a few sheep, and a hippo missing a leg. She is taking them for a walk in the "woods" and feeding them mushrooms. The legs of the chairs are her trees, the brown edge of the carpet is a dirt path.

I grab our suitcases, meaning to unpack. As I walk into my bed-room, Dave follows.

"We need to talk face-to-face tonight," he says.

Scott said to cease contact.

"What's it regarding?" I ask. He won't give me specifics. "Without details, I can't agree to meet with you." I step around him.

He keeps following me, repeating his request.

"We're going to email only," I tell him. "You can send me the budget I've been waiting for. And I need my money for January."

"I can't write you a check until we talk."

I try to step around him again, remembering that Scott said in order to protect myself financially, I have to file for divorce. I feel trapped. "Stop blocking me. You're being a bully."

He smirks. "Call the police if you want." I ignore him and he puts one arm across the doorway. "You're not going to deliver edicts to me!"

Then he drops his arm and, in a different tone, says, "Come on. This is me."

I squint at him. "Oh yeah? Who *are* you anyway?"

Dave sighs and becomes Mr. Reasonable. He starts expounding on the benefits of mediation, how it will save time and money, and how he knows that *I don't want to be the one* to make this difficult.

"There's no point going to mediation if you're not going to be forthright," I say. "You need to show me financial records."

He doesn't respond.

"You also need to let me know your thoughts on a parenting schedule."

"We'll discuss all that in mediation," he says.

Stalemate. I hoist my suitcase on the bed and try to focus on unpacking, but Dave remains in the door, watching me, unnerving me. I push past him and go to the kitchen, where I start opening cabinets randomly. Finally he leaves and I hear the dining room chair creak as he sits down in front of his computer. I open the refrigerator, only to find it bare. As I stand staring at its cold emptiness, a cold emptiness rumbles in me and I too feel plugged in, humming with electric current. I slam the fridge door and stride to the dining room.

"There aren't any groceries. I need money to go get some."

"I'll take care of the kids today."

"*I'm* hungry."

He levels a look at me. "There's some salad in there."

I feel trapped in this house, this situation, this mess. I stare at Dave a moment, and then I shout as loudly as I can, "Can! I! Have! Some! Money! Please?"

I feel rather than see April go still under the table. Dave reaches for his wallet so fast that I actually step back. He hands me $60, a small smile on his face. He's happy to see me acting the crazy lady. Tammy losing her composure translates to a free pass for him. I suppose I should be more careful now, but I can't. I *feel* crazy.

I snatch the money and go back to my room, and that's when I notice that the bedspread is disheveled. I move the suitcase and look more closely. The pillows are rearranged. This is not the way I left this bed. In a flash, I'm back to the table, standing over Dave.

"Were you in my room while I was gone?"

He shrugs. "Yeah. I slept in there."

"Did you have anyone in there with you?"

He shakes his head and grimaces as if I'm so silly. "Of course not."

I slap him, hard, across the face. He rears back, shocked, one cheek pink, the other red.

"Don't you ever hit me again!" he sputters.

My words hiss, low and fiery. "Don't you tell me what to do. And if you *ever* put your filthy body in my bed or go in my room again, I will kill you."

Here it is. The war zone. I've hit another person, something I thought I'd never do, and I don't care. Worse, I would do it again.

And April is there, underneath the table, like a mushroom in the forest. A silent little sponge.

After dinner with Abigail, I come home to find Dave sitting on the living room sofa, waiting for me.

"You don't need to file for dissipation of assets," he says.

My eyes dart to the dining room table, my heart sinking before I even see it: my laptop, open. He's seen my email exchanges with Scott.

I stay calm. "I'm following the advice of my attorney."

"If you're trying to stop me from making my album, that was planned a long time ago."

I know that Dave wrote a check for nearly $4,000 right before he closed our joint checking account, but I don't know what else he has spent.

"How much is that costing?" I ask.

"I'm going to have to borrow another $4,000 from Alex." His tone is accusatory. "You bought those plane tickets to Nashville without asking me." Indicating the room around us, he adds, "And the money you spent on those decorators. . . ."

Ah. Those decorators. I recall the wonderful glow I felt on Thanksgiving as we gathered with our friends in this room; what I thought of as blessings are now called assets.

"Recording an album probably isn't a priority when we're going through a divorce," I remind him.

"That's not your call. I budgeted for the album."

"Did you budget for the escorts? How much did you spend on that little hobby?"

He waves his hand. "A negligible amount! Hardly anything."

"So give me a number."

He doesn't answer.

"You're going to have to account for it."

"You don't account for every cent you spend."

I choose my next words carefully. "In light of recent events and information you've given me, it seems reasonable that you have to provide some figures and that your, *our*, assets be frozen."

"Do you hear how you sound?" he asks.

I do hear it, my "you're-so-stupid" tone, but I'm angry, and I don't know how to express anger. Condescension is something I can manage. I sigh, drop my purse on the floor and sit across from him.

After a long silence, he says, tentatively, "How do you envision the possibility of us staying together?"

"How do you envision it?"

"I want to be myself," he says.

"But who is that? Who exactly are you?"

"You know me better than anyone."

I look at him, confused. This needs to stop. I should go to bed and save these conversations for a therapist. Attempting to talk is no less dangerous than juggling chainsaws. If there were a TV screen in this room it would be flashing *Do not attempt this at home!*

Dave begins to cry. "I'm scared to death of being alone, of you and the kids hating me."

I freeze. I've never been good at witnessing Dave in crisis. The Dave I thought I knew was a rock, governed by pragmatism and steadfastness. He's not one to succumb to emotionalism, and I wonder if that's the way he really is, or is it that he never gets emotional because I don't know how to react? I study my hands.

"You've never actually asked for forgiveness."

"I did! I have! I'm very sorry. Can you forgive me?"

Finally, an apology! But I feel nothing. I stall, wondering what's wrong with me that I can't accept this and be satisfied. What do I expect? What would be enough?

"What does forgiveness mean to you?" I wait, searching his face, but it reveals nothing.

"I'm not going to crawl on my knees."

I'm so tired. The painful truth is that we don't know how to communicate. Over the years, our pattern has been to have this back and forth game of he-said, she-said. We are always recapping our fights instead of having them. Maybe it's the scribe in both of us that we fight over the script and are never able to name the drama. If we were superheroes, we would have capes covered with giant type and we would *wordsmith* each other to death.

Dave stands. "You have a week to contact a mediator."

I watch him go, and in the blank of his retreating back, I glimpse a language I finally understand. He's already gone, and has been gone a very long time. The next morning I'm on LaSalle Street in downtown Chicago, on the thirty-second floor of a gleaming, vault-like building. It's been exactly six weeks since we had Thanksgiving dinner with Dave's family. Scott pushes a paper in front of me, hands me a pen, and without hesitating I sign my name on a petition for divorce.

9 The Buddha at My Table

Anger is a living thing, a kind of protozoon, single-celled at first but multiplying at an alarming rate, with a life and mobility all its own. I feel powerless over it in the same way I seem unable to stop spores of mold from growing in my tub. Still, I try to take control in small ways.

First, I schedule an AIDS and STD test and tell Dave that he has to do the same. He responds agreeably, as if this were routine—just a pleasant, yearly checkup.

"Where are you taking it?" he asks.

"At the nurse-midwives group." Again I sense an expectation, as if I'm supposed to arrange this too for him. I think, *make your own damn appointment! It can't be any harder than finding escorts!* I bite my tongue, but the flare of rage I feel frightens me. It's unpredictable and blazes through me like a gas can catching fire.

Next, I sign the order for temporary support that Scott prepares, relieved to have a piece of paper ordering Dave to deposit a set amount of money into my account twice a month. Having dispensed with these business items, I tackle an emotional one. I take down my wedding albums one night, while Dave is out, and Abigail and I look through them. This is done with a veneer of control. I tell myself the pain is like being vaccinated—quick, but strengthening over the long haul. That's not true. It's like getting a flu shot when you're dying of cancer. It's pointless, desperate, delusional.

One thing is certain: Dave is not reminiscing on our wedding vows. He gets in at 2:30 a.m. I hear him in the bathroom before he goes downstairs to the sofa. As I lie in bed, wide awake, listening, it's like a magnet flips over in me. Where my thoughts and feelings were pulling me toward him—*When will Dave be home? Will he talk to me? Will he listen to me?*—they are now pushing away. Things are sinking in a little more each day. He's just devastated his family and he's been at a fucking office party. The cruelty, the callousness, leave me cold. I am finally going from *How could he do this to me?* to He. Did. *This.* To. *Me.*

I wake up afraid. My friends and family are so close to me now, comforting me. What will happen when this becomes old news? People will turn back to their busy lives. I'll be alone and forgotten.

The weather doesn't help. It's cold and dreary, the air heavy with doom. Before I can drive the kids to school, I have to scrape the ice from the van windows. There's a thin layer of ice on the inside, too. I'm like this, icy inside and out, frozen at the thought of Dave and me seeing Mary tonight. I can't do this, I think. But what choice do I have? I have to keep going. That means getting the kids to school, feeding them, feeding myself. My stomach lurches at the thought of food, and then, serendipitously, I open the console in the van to find a bag of sliced apples. Cathy gave them to me the day I visited her and I'd forgotten them. I nibble on one. Honey crisps, cold and sweet, with a blast of tartness that makes my eyes water. I wish that just once I could get through the school drop-off line without having to hide my tear-stained face from the other moms.

That night, getting ready for the therapy session, I'm anxious and depressed and snapping at the kids. They want dinner. Correction, they want ice cream. *Fine!* I say. *Have it!*

I'm in the bedroom when I hear the babysitter arrive.

A few minutes later Logan bursts in. "Mom, there's a man in an orange cape sitting at the dining room table!"

I walk through the kitchen and, indeed, there's a Buddhist monk, bald and be-robed, sitting there quietly. My babysitter introduces him as her friend. They're both Thai, and he doesn't speak English.

I offer him something to drink and the babysitter answers for him. "He is very happy with tea," she says.

When I place the teacup before him, he smiles and nods enthusiastically. Smiling in return, I say goodbye, probably too loudly, as I back out the door. I take his presence as a message, because really, how many people have had a monk at their table? Maybe he's here to encourage a Zen-like detachment in me, but it's not getting through the raging hatefulness I feel.

I recall something that author and Buddhist monk Thich Nhat Hanh wrote about anger, that venting does nothing but train one in aggression, that the trick to dissolving the knots of anger is to recognize them, then embrace them with awareness and tenderness. He gives this meditation: *Breathing in, I know that anger has manifested in me. Breathing out, I smile toward my anger.*

I repeat this mantra as I take my seat on Mary's sofa. Dave is already there, sitting at the other end. Mary waits for us to start. I wait too, unwilling to facilitate.

"I'm sorry I broke our contract and went outside our marriage," Dave says. He adds that he's sorry about Allison and that he won't mention her name again until the divorce is final.

Gee, thanks. It's been five minutes and there's a pressure in me building so quickly that I don't dare open my mouth. Smiling is out of the question.

Dave points at my unopened water bottle. He says he left his water in the car. Can he have mine? I give it to him. He takes a quick drink before continuing.

"After I had my heart broken in college I swore I would never let that happen again, so I chose someone who wouldn't break my heart."

"What are you talking about?" I get that I'm the one who is no heart-breaker, but who is this college girlfriend? He's spoken about a couple of long-term girlfriends but never revealed any deep scars they may have left.

"I've never felt passionately in love with you," he says.

Maybe this should cut me, but it doesn't. Did I think we were passionately in love? No. Do I know many people who are? No. We're in our forties! We certainly had our early years of being inseparable, and our sex life was, at least by comparisons gleaned through the girlfriend network, pretty regular and average. I thought that passion was the stuff of movies and epic novels. I'm more practical and realistic. I've always felt a strong friendship and a like-mindedness in interests, attitudes, and sensibilities. I chose what I needed most, someone solid and steadfast and fair-minded. Someone whose intelligence I admired, who inspired me with his creative thinking. These are the bricks that build a sturdy structure. Passion is the colorful wall paint that fades and chips over time. To hear Dave focus on passion leaves me baffled.

"This doesn't make sense," I say. "I know you loved me. You're rewriting history to suit yourself."

"That's not it. Yes, I felt genuine feelings, and it was real for me, but now I want something different."

"I'm trying to understand what you want. Is this really about some great love? Are you trying to say Allison is the love of your life? You spent twelve hours together! What about the escorts?"

"I don't know that I believe in monogamy."

This *does* cut me. Monogamy is my bedrock. Dave's words are a blast that topples everything.

"Let me get this straight. You want to find some great love to make you feel constantly desired, understood, etcetera, and at the same time have casual sex?"

He shrugs. "Maybe."

I look at Mary incredulously. "That's crazy!"

She says, "Tammy, you are certainly in the majority, but there is a minority of people who have open relationships and make it work."

I turn back to this person I've known for twenty years. "That's what you want, Dave?"

He seems to be sinking into the sofa. "Maybe."

"Sure, you'll find that in the land of unicorns," I snap.

Mary interjects. "We could be dealing with a sex addiction. Is that possible?"

Dave doesn't deny it and something in me clicks shut.

"Dave talks like a battered wife," Mary says, "like he's afraid of you. It makes him all mumbly and impossible to understand, and of course leads to you being frustrated and confused." She turns to him. "Stop acting like the bad guy. Take ownership of your wants and actions."

Dave sits straighter. "I'd like to wrap things up in the next four weeks. I don't want to draw this out."

White hot fury blinds me. I want to leap at him and claw his eyes out. I want to call him every name in the book. I look to Mary again. Can't she see how crazy Dave is? Can't she *do* something?

"Why don't you tell Tammy more about how you decided this?" Mary says. "Why you told her the way you did."

"I wanted you to hear all of it so you could see the finality of it, that it wasn't just something that came up suddenly. It's been there a long time."

Mary suggests that I work on a concrete list of things I need from Dave. Her briskness implies a finality, and I see it. I get it. But it's like viewing a dead body that's still warm. Surely there should be time to sit shiva. But not when Mary's clock is ticking at the rate of two dollars a minute. I ask for a phone bill. Dave shakes his head.

"You said you hate to see me torturing myself. Then give me something to verify what you've told me."

He doesn't budge.

"You're asking me to give you a divorce, to give up my entire life and hopes for the future. I'm asking you for a fucking phone bill."

Mary wants to wrap things up, too. "Work on a parenting schedule," she says. "You can start dividing time right away."

This makes Dave uncomfortable. He voices concern about telling the kids and the effect it will have on them.

"It's documented that kids lose a year, both academically and emotionally, even in amicable divorces," Mary says evenly. I can see that Dave is stunned, and so am I. She also mentions that one couple she worked with spent $300,000 on their divorce. I wonder if this is her neutral way of giving Dave a reality check, like *Wake up, you idiot!*

I've had enough of her neutrality and pussy-footing around. I'm not putting myself through this again. Leaving, I feel an anger so explosive I have trouble getting the key in the ignition of my car with my shaking hands. How dare Dave say he doesn't want to draw this out? He's had ten years to consider this and make his unilateral choices. Now I sit through one session where I'm told we don't have enough passion and that he doesn't believe in monogamy, and I'm supposed to accept this? I can't see straight as I drive, and I consider pulling over. But the last thing I need is to sit and stew in a stalled car the way I'm stewing in my stalled life. I know that there is no going back. I have to go forward.

I get home long before Dave. The monk has gone. There's the chair where he sat, a visitor in a foreign land, not speaking the language, smiling because he had a cup of tea. It's the same chair I sat in that night, when Dave called me to the table. This chair has held both my shock and a monk's peace. I touch the seat. If there's anything there now, I don't feel it. All I feel are knots of anger. There's no dissolving them, no embracing them with tenderness. I want to vent. I want to destroy something, anything. I want to die.

10 When I Grow Up

I arrive at my next session with Walter overwhelmed by the venomous thoughts poisoning me lately. I expect to deliver a strike against Dave, but as often happens, once I'm in this quiet room looking into Walter's placid, patient face, I open my mouth and unexpected things come out.

"Why do family patterns repeat?" I ask. "Do we always attract what we fear? How do we get off the gerbil wheel and break these patterns for our kids?"

"We could talk about that," Walter says, "or other philosophical, esoteric topics. Or we could talk about how you're feeling."

This makes me cry. Dammit. I thought I was angry. I'm ready to be angry. But I'm so sad. I just want my friend back. It's like going through some terrible shock that you know only your best friend can make better, and then there's this sinking realization. Oh. *Right.* He's not my friend anymore. And there's no time to get used to it.

"I wonder if he misses me," I manage to say. "He had time to prepare for this, and he decided that I'm expendable."

"It must feel very lonely."

I cry harder. "I always imagined myself alone one day. I had a gut feeling that it would be because of Dave dying first. By then I'd be a strong old woman." I laugh tearfully. "Do you know the Michelle Shocked song called *When I Grow up I Want to be an Old Woman?*"

Walter shakes his head.

"Well, Dave knows it. It's . . . I don't know how to explain. It's the simple things. Like this pet peeve I have; I hate feeling a draft on my back when I'm sleeping. My pajamas have to be covering my back, and the covers need to be in place. Weird, I know, but I told Dave to remember this. I wanted him to promise to always cover my back."

I pause, unable to continue. Walter waits.

"You get it?" I finally ask.

"Who will cover your back?"

I nod, diving for the Kleenex. "When you're married, you get to have that. You get to be a cozy old woman."

"That's one picture. But there are others. You said your grandmother was alone for many years. And your mother is alone. They must be very independent."

"I don't want to be like them!"

"What about your dad? He's married to his fifth wife, right? So do you think you're the only one who doesn't want to be alone? Don't you think it's natural to feel this way, especially now, when it's not something you saw coming?"

"That's my point, though. Does it matter if we see it or not? People seem destined to repeat their parents' patterns."

"We're getting into analysis again. What are you feeling?"

"Confused." I begin shredding the Kleenex in my hand. "Dave says he doesn't want to draw this out, but now he's making custody demands that don't make sense. He wants me to give up the kids half the time, even though I'm at home and he works full time. Why should I have to do that? Why should I have to be without my kids at all when this is his choice?"

"What do you choose?"

"Does it matter? I don't have a say in any of this."

"Is that true?"

"Well, I certainly can't choose to believe him because I know he's still lying to me. Just the other day I had to look through his files. My lawyer said to collect all these documents. So I sneaked into the office while Dave was at work. My heart was pounding. I was so worried I wouldn't find anything, sick to my stomach thinking I would."

"What did you find?"

"There was a folder marked Las Vegas with a color brochure for a strip club. Why would he file that away? And I saw that all the financial files stop at 2006."

"And yet Dave said he was sorry he broke your contract."

I'm quiet a moment. "Okay, I get it."

"Apologies are nice but ultimately meaningless when not backed up by behavior," Walter says. "Dave would have to be willing to pick up every broken piece and hold it up for you to see. And be willing to let you look at each one for as long as you need to. That's remorse. He's not showing any of that. Neither has your dad."

I can't imagine either of them ever doing that. "Dave says it's complicated," I offer feebly. "I wouldn't understand."

"Tammy, you write novels. You make up entire lives, characters, motivations, dialogue. What could be so complicated that you wouldn't understand?"

I don't know what to say to this.

"Are you writing about this experience?"

"Journaling, yes. But not anything else. I can't concentrate. There are too many emotions. Too much to think about." Tears threaten again. "And it's so unfair! Just when I was getting back to writing. I had started a short story, and I have an idea for a new novel too. Now I don't see how I'll ever be able to write again."

"Say more about that."

"I have to say goodbye to fiction, don't I? I'll have to write this goddamn story of Dave and me, whether I like it or not, because this is what I've been given. It's like a prison sentence."

"And. . . .?"

I look at him blankly.

"What's the feeling?"

"I feel cheated, attacked, like I need to defend myself and try to reason with Dave, and—"

"Those aren't feelings. What's the feeling? Anger! Feel it."

"I'm afraid to."

Walter nods. "You like to have a sort of cognitive map in order to analyze and find answers. That's a good tool for a writer. But you move into labeling so quickly that you don't feel the emotion. And as I've said before, as soon as you label an experience, you stop having it."

"I don't understand."

"The body is where wisdom and mystery live. You can't out-think everything. When a situation arises that makes you angry, it means your body needs to feel anger. Think of the strong emotions as clearing space for you to live your purpose. To write. It's like cleaning a basement. Throw things out, don't examine everything."

"That seems an oxymoron for a writer."

"Live it first, then write it."

"I could experiment with that."

"Writing is not your experiment," Walter says slowly. "It's who you are."

No one has ever said those words to me, yet it's what I've always known. I feel stabbed in the heart, weak with gratitude.

"How do you know that?"

"Because you told me."

"But why do you believe me?"

Walter only smiles.

11 The Questions

One day, passing Dave in the kitchen, I break my own rule of non-engagement by asking, "Do you have anything you want to talk to me about?"

He gives me a blank look. "No, is there something you want to talk to me about?"

I hesitate. "I have the distinct feeling that you have other bombs to drop and it's really stressful waiting around. I'd rather you tell me now."

"I don't have any bombs to drop."

"You had a bag of clothes . . . "

"That's for a photo shoot. For work."

"Okay. Well, it's a number of things. I don't know whether you're going to disappear one day, and the kids will be confused."

"I told you that's not going to happen."

I shake my head. "You haven't told me anything. I have no idea what you're planning."

He leans back against the counter and crosses his arms. "I said I want to go to mediation."

Dave has brought up mediation repeatedly, but I don't see the point when I don't know when or if he's lying. Mediation needs a measure of good faith on both sides, something we don't have. I remind him of this.

"Let's talk about bird-nesting then," he says.

"No way. Not happening."

"Then I should move upstairs," he says.

"And kick the tenant out? What about his lease? What about the fact that I don't want you living over my head? Jeez, if you want a divorce, we're getting a divorce. We're not sharing a house!"

"I could promise to not have anyone over for a year."

"Why would you keep that promise?"

"We could put it in a legal document."

"Legal like a marriage contract?"

Dave's face hardens. "You need to listen to me. We're going to discuss these things. You can't—"

"Stop! I gave you my answer. Now you're badgering and bullying me. This is what you do when you don't get your way, and it's not going to work anymore. I won't put myself in a position to trust you again."

He says nothing more, but the look he gives me makes me turn away. I rush to the bathroom and lean, shaken, against the closed door. I feel stunned, as if I've seen a ghost because just then, in the waning afternoon light, with shadows reaching toward him, Dave's face slid into an expression eerily familiar. It was my father, as clear as a photograph, with the same hostile stare, the same set of the jaw. The child within my heart is crushed and so is the image I've been holding of Dave. I know I will never see him the same way again. But worse than that, I looked at his face and felt some strangled, odd surge of love. God, please not that! I don't know where to put that.

Where do I put the love?

I toss and turn all that night. Finally, at 6:00 a.m., I go downstairs and wake Dave.

"I don't know what to do," I say, kneeling beside the sofa. "If there's any chance of staying together, we have to try."

He rubs his face sleepily, then sits up.

"There are things I can't even share with you."

"Like what?" I do a frantic mental check, spinning through the years for a clue to some untoward predilection Dave may have shown. I don't want to go there. Apparently Dave doesn't either.

Without looking at me, he says, "Maybe for the sake of the kids we should try to reconcile. I've been thinking about it constantly."

This should make me feel hopeful, but it has the opposite effect. How long have I been auditioning for my marriage without knowing? Not even for a starring role, for my sake, but for a chance to be in the background, like a prop in the corner. And yet, the children do deserve center stage.

"If you want me to be a different person, someone open to . . . to . . . other arrangements, that's not going to work. You know me and my values."

Dave doesn't answer. We sit in a roomful of questions. We sit for what seems forever. Rainer Maria Rilke, in *Letters to a Young Poet*, writes, "Don't search for the answers, which could not be given to you now, because you would not be able to live them. And the point is to live everything. Live the questions now."

I don't want to live this. I want some sort of answer, from someone. I think of my friend, Danielle, who is a therapist.

"Dave, Danielle gave me the name of someone in her practice she thinks can help us. Her name is Claudette. Will you go?"

The sound he makes is unintelligible. I interpret it as yes.

Claudette is an older woman who walks with a cane. She wears her red hair swept up and balances bifocals on the end of her nose. Her office is small; a simple sofa faces her wing back chair. Dave and I sit across from her and when she asks what brings us in, Dave turns to me, as if I'm going to start. I say nothing. Let's see what he's got!

Finally he says, "Two things: a systemic lack of passion and a growing contempt and resentment on Tammy's part."

I look at Claudette. Clearly she needs some context. I give her a one-sentence summary of Dave's confessions and his request for a divorce. Then I turn to him.

"Contempt? Really?"

"Yes."

"I honestly did not know how you were feeling. You never said anything."

"That's not true. You had to know I was unhappy."

"I had no idea!"

Claudette says, "Your two completely different versions of reality are confusing."

"Listening to him confuses me," I say. "Everything he says is so contradictory."

"I committed to being the best husband and father I could be."

"How do the escorts fit in with that?" Claudette asks.

"That's separate," Dave insists. "It never affected Tammy or our family."

She nods. "So what are we doing here?" She lets the silence grow, then asks, "Did you betray your wife?"

Dave hesitates. "Yes, and no. Yes by conventional standards, but I wasn't taking away from what we had."

"I'm not sure what conventions apply here. Can you explain that?"

"It didn't affect anyone else. I gave her one hundred percent."

I look down at myself. Either I'm invisible or I can't do basic math. "But you betrayed others as well. My family, our friends . . . "

"You're the one who told everyone."

I throw my hands up. Claudette addresses Dave. "There seems to be an issue of impulse control and a pattern of risk-taking that has been increasingly dangerous."

Dave shakes his head. "I knew I wouldn't get caught."

"And yet you chose to tell Tammy everything."

"I wanted her to know that we were definitely over."

Claudette nods. "And you say that your infidelity began more than ten years ago?"

"The first affair was only a blip. It was actually most challenging for me because there were feelings involved."

Her brow furrows. "So was that affair a blip or a difficult decision?"

Dave considers this. "Both, I guess. The escorts were my way of not being tempted with emotional attachment."

She looks at me but I have nothing to add. After a deep breath, she says, "I appreciate that you were both so honest with me. Now I have a responsibility to be honest with you. I've never had to say this before in all my years of practice, but I will not be able to help because, frankly Dave, I can't understand you." She takes her glasses off and leans toward him. "There are three people in the room and two of us do not know what you are trying to say. You're contradictory, and no reasonable person could be expected to follow your logic. I need to support and respect both of you equally as my clients, and while I believe I could respect that you believe what you're saying, I simply can't find one shred of real honesty to work with. I also do not detect a bond between you, or a glimmer of hope to work with."

She puts her glasses back on. "Tammy, I'm sorry."

I feel a momentary shock, as if a Band-Aid has been ripped off, then a cool rush of air, surprisingly soothing. Claudette stands and I spring to my feet as well. As we say goodbye, Dave is polite and thanks her. At the elevator he says, "That was just as I expected. That woman wasn't objective at all. You must be so happy to be validated by your friend's colleague."

"Yes, I'm so happy to be told there's nothing to work with, that someone had to turn us away because there's no hope for us. I'm thrilled by that." The truth is that I am, if not exactly thrilled, relieved. I'm not crazy, as Dave would have me believe.

His face is hard. "You'll have a great story to tell all your gossipy friends now."

Story—the theme of our wedding. The stuff of life, as our "narrator" John said that day. The context that gives all experience meaning. The elevator takes us down, and I turn my back to Dave and probe my wounds, only to find that the sting has lessened. I've lived this and I'm done. Ready to face a blank page.

12 The Princess

Two months have passed since Dave sat across from me at the dining room table and woke me from my dream with all the finesse of a machete hacking through bramble. Prince Charming he wasn't. And I am still under a curse—awake, yet sleepwalking through my days. The thorn pricking me lately is that the kids don't know what's happening. Dave and I have not agreed on the best time to tell them we're divorcing.

He doesn't hesitate, however, to surprise me by announcing that he's taking the kids to Disney World for spring break. We went with the boys once, when I was seven months pregnant with April, and while a good dose of pirates, Tom Sawyer, and Space Mountain was fun, *my* Fantasyland is Cinderella's Castle, the Prince Charming Regal Carrousel, Belle, and The Little Mermaid—all things I want to experience with my four-year-old daughter. I *have* to have this. Dave has no right to take it from me.

The judge doesn't see it that way. In one of our first court battles, my attorney Scott argues that spending money on a trip to Disney is not a wise financial decision, but the judge believes Dave when he says he can afford it; he gives him permission to take the trip. In the hallway afterward, Scott and I square off with Dave and his attorney.

"Every kid has a right to go to Disney," Dave's attorney says. "Why would you take that from them?"

"Let's be real here," Scott says. "Your client has a history of irresponsible spending."

Dave's attorney ignores Scott and addresses me. "Your kids should not have to suffer by not going to Disney. Besides, if everyone waited until they had the money to take a vacation, well, we'd never have anything, would we?"

"Do you mean to say that any kid who doesn't go to Disney is suffering?" I ask.

"They're entitled to a good vacation," he says. "That's what credit cards are for."

"That may be what you do with your money," I say angrily, "but we don't—"

Scott interjects. "That's your advice, counselor?"

"My client will charge it," he tells Scott with a shrug. "Like yours does when she buys herself a pair of shoes or has her nails done."

I gape at him and at Dave, who says nothing. He's under a curse as well, and as this story begins its long careening toward the end, a sense of foreboding falls across the land.

I'm dressing one morning when it hits me with the clarity of a thunderclap that it's time to tell the kids. *Now.* Maybe it's the simple act of reaching for a lighter sweater. Spring is springing, it's a whole new season, and yet the children have been frozen in a cold state of confusion. They've been told simply that Mom and Dad aren't getting along and need some time away from each other, but it's one thing to have us sleep in separate rooms, and quite another to fly to Florida without their mother. Whether four or forty, it doesn't make sense.

It's a weekday, but they don't have school, so I'm alone with them all day. A certainty grows in me. I know that conventional wisdom says to tell them together, as a unit. But what happened to maternal intuition? To knowing what's right for me and my own kids? I text Dave. He says he has "plans" and won't be home that night. He warns me to think about what I'm doing. But I have thought. It's time to act.

I've already talked to Walter about this possibility. Now I call Abigail. She says, impatiently, "Why is this so drawn out? And when have you been able to count on him to be anything but manipulative?"

That afternoon, I call Logan and Jed and April into the living room and ask, "How do you feel about going to Florida with just Dad? Do you think it's odd?"

They've arranged themselves in order in front of the sofa, like descending stair steps, with Logan at the top. I have a bizarre urge to rub each of their heads. I knead my hands together.

"Since Dad and I still aren't getting along, it's not possible for me to go."

Logan blurts, "You're not getting divorced, are you?"

I blink, stunned. Then breathe. "Well honey, we're thinking about it, yes."

He bursts into tears.

"Why is Logan crying?" Jed asks. April is silent and wide-eyed.

I reach for Logan's hand and wait for his tears to stop.

"When Mom and Dad got married, we thought it would be forever. But sometimes things change. A marriage is kind of like a recipe and it needs certain ingredients. Without the right ingredients, a marriage won't work. So some things have changed, and some important things are missing now, and that means we can't stay together." I take Jed's hand too. "But even though our feelings have changed for each other, the good part is that parents' feelings for their kids never change. We'll always be your mom and dad and we'll always love you."

The uncertainty on their faces makes me falter. My eyes well with tears. "It's a very sad time for us all, but it's a new beginning, and we'll always have each other and our friends. We'll always be a family." I wish I'd thought to grab a Kleenex. I swipe at my cheeks. "Remember, God watches over us and has a plan for all of us."

I give them each a crushing hug. As Walter predicted, they have the attention span of gnats, and want to go play. My relief is enormous and somewhat perplexing. It reminds me of my first heartbreak, at sixteen, when my boyfriend dumped me. Before the pain hit, there was a window of relief that came close to happiness. His distant behavior had confused me and raised a tsunami of self-doubt. The fact that he told me, face-to-face, that he wanted to break up was strangely exhilarating and restored my dignity. I feel a similar satisfaction now about speaking to my kids in my own language about my values without Dave, like an emotional black hole, siphoning my confidence.

Logan seems to feel the same wabi-sabi relief. He brings it up later, saying he isn't happy, but he isn't sad either.

I inform Dave of our conversation via a text, and he is absolutely not happy. He cuts his evening plans short and just before the kids go to bed, he gathers everyone and tells them again that we are divorcing. They have nothing to say.

The next morning Logan comes into the kitchen smiling. "I feel better than I have, and I think it's because, you know, you guys are getting divorced. I can't explain it. I feel better than I have in my whole life."

I set a slice of toast in front of him. "It probably feels good to know what's going on. It's not healthy living with a secret."

He chews for a while, deep in thought. Finally he announces, "Mom, I know why you're getting divorced."

I raise my eyebrows, waiting.

"Because of the economy."

I smile and this time I do rub his head.

13 My Whole Heart

Once the lawyers have been dispatched, I settle in for a long wait. I've been warned that the divorce process requires the patience of Job. I've heard this phrase many times, but what exactly does it mean? The Bible describes Job as a righteous man who lost all his children and earthly possessions in one day, and then suffered festering sores over his entire body. Rather than cursing God, Job looked past his suffering and emotionalism and held to his deeper beliefs, that God is sovereign, and God is good. As one who curses loudly at the first tingle of a cold sore, I have to work to get my head around this. And getting my head to work is *work*. I'm at the mercy of my heart now, and it's demanding to take the lead.

It leads me to online dating. This is my version of showing faith, so I ignore the desperation that hovers annoyingly over my shoulder, fuel my resolve with two glasses of red wine, and lash out a profile late one night. My headline reads *Are You Awake?* and it's only later that I see how pretentious this sounds. My description is equally cringe-worthy, beginning with the words "Fit, active mom." *Horrible.* It sounds like a casting call for a laundry detergent commercial. But, as luck has it, I come across a profile that intrigues without intimidating. A man named Paul has three children the same age as mine and also went to Indiana University when I did. It's a start, and I shoot a friendly email pointing out these commonalities. We exchange a few successful messages and then make a date to talk on the phone.

It's a Wednesday night when I dial Paul's number from a nearby bookstore. Dave and I still don't have an official parenting schedule. He remains entrenched in the basement and if he has plans to move out soon, he hasn't shared them. He comes and goes as he chooses—mostly goes. But I've set aside Wednesday nights as "my time" which so far has consisted of wandering Target or listlessly performing unimportant errands. Now I find an empty chair stuffed between the shelves, press myself into a corner, and turn my face toward the books. I look decidedly suspicious, as if I'm the one about to embark on a clandestine affair. I have to remind myself that I've been set free (not *left*) and try to kindle the feeling that this is a good thing. Before Paul can pick up I'm already convinced that this is a waste of time. But I haven't dated in twenty years, and I have to start somewhere. With a deep breath, I decide to treat this as practice.

Paul has a nice voice. He talks with a folksy drawl that reminds me of Jimmy Stewart. It's only when he says he's an accountant that I hear a sort of *wanh-wanh-wahn*, like in a cartoon when the cat snatches the money bag and makes his getaway, only to look inside and find it empty—oh rats! I don't let it stop me. I think of my friend Susan, a fellow writer, who dated an accountant. She said it was fun to be the creative one. Besides, it's not as if this is going to go anywhere.

We chat about our kids, our home towns, our respective marital statuses. Paul has recently finalized his divorce and seems accepting of my not-so-separate separation and the fact that Dave lives in the same house. Divorcing is a long process, Paul says. Likely two years. This startles me so much that I choose to ignore it. Eventually the bookstore becomes distracting so I walk back to my car and drive home as we continue our conversation. Just as I'm beginning to enjoy the slow, thoughtful way he talks and the way his smile comes through the line, his energy changes and he pauses.

"I have to admit something," he says.

Dread clutches at my heart. He had an affair. I'm sure of it. Never mind that no one in the history of dating has ever confessed such a thing in the first thirty minutes. What else could it possibly be?

"I have multiple sclerosis," he says. "I usually don't tell people that until after we meet, but it feels good to be open about it."

I'm relieved—is that all?—until it sinks in: serious incurable disease. I hesitate. "How does it affect you?"

"I have weakness on my left side. I can walk but sometimes it tires me out, so I use a wheelchair to go longer distances."

I don't know much about multiple sclerosis so I'm not sure what to say. He says that his normal date routine is to arrive at the restaurant early, stow his wheelchair, and then wait for the right time to tell his date about it.

"That sounds stressful."

"You have no idea. Thank you."

I laugh uncomfortably. "For what?"

"I'm not sure exactly. I just feel I can be honest with you."

Something different clutches at my heart then, something I can't name. Suddenly bashful, I mumble that I've arrived at my house and had better get inside. I turn off my car and step onto the sidewalk that runs beside my front fence.

"What do you have going on tomorrow?" Paul asks and I'm stopped in my tracks. I grab the fence, unsteady. How long has it been since Dave has asked how I spend my days? For a moment, however fleetingly, someone cares. It gives me hope. But later, alone in bed, staring at my ceiling, I think of what I'll be doing the next day and the day after and how many different roles I'll play. Hopelessness descends. How could someone new ever know all the sides of me? Would it be weird for me to write up character sketches about myself?

The Grieving Wife craves peanut butter and orange juice in the night, like when she was pregnant. She relives that time, remembering her joy, and then it turns sour as she realizes her husband had already cheated. She cries for more than an hour as her history unravels and rewrites itself into something sordid and tainted. Her friend Abigail says, "He can't take that from you. You feel it's ruined but you were living fully and authentically, happy to be carrying the baby of the man you loved. Your whole heart was engaged in that reality, and he will never have that. How sad for him."

The Floundering Mom wants to get a dog for her kids. Okay, maybe for herself. Her husband, who is leaving her, tells her no. "Do you think it's legal for you to get a dog if I don't want one?" he asks. But she craves something small, clean, devoted. At the shelter, she and the kids are lucky enough to find a toy poodle. Her hand shakes filling out the application. She knows the rules: all members of the household are required to be present. When the adoption counselor asks if the entire family is there, she says yes, but her son pipes up, "No, not Daddy! And he's the one who doesn't want a dog." The counselor calls her into the hallway. She fumbles her explanation, feeling like she just tried to steal the crown jewels. The counselor listens but says Dad will have to be called. As the kids play with the dog, she attempts to downplay her embarrassment and sense of being judged. Divorced people are failures. They can't commit. They don't know how to love. They certainly don't deserve dogs. But the counselor comes back and says that Dad has begrudgingly agreed. The kids lead the dog to the car and she follows, victorious but strangely sad. She wanted small, clean, devoted. Instead she feels unwieldy, messy, bereft.

The Angry, Fed-Up Petitioner in Cook County case docket number D02-99 receives a court order to see a vocational expert and unleashes her outrage in a sarcastic blog she calls *The Color of My Parachute*. She writes that her husband Dave is so kind to bring the matter of her unemployment before a judge. It's not uncommon, she's told, for a working husband to demand a job evaluation, but she knows of only one other person—her cousin—who was "invited" to career counseling. Her cousin's ex-husband is a prince, a successful hotshot who had it all, including a pregnant girlfriend in Mexico. Her cousin was tested and questioned and evaluated and told she might make a good office manager. Instead, she's taking anatomy and biology on her way to becoming a registered nurse, which is a shame, because she makes a mean cup of coffee.

This wife is a writer. She has a bachelor's degree somewhere, but that's a vague memory, made murky by years of lactating and other mom stuff. And what do moms really do anyway? She heard on the radio that if you assign a market value to each of a mom's duties, she would earn a salary of $118,000. Ha! A conspiracy theory, no doubt, started by lazy, unqualified whiners who want credit for living the easy life. Not her. She's *eager* to be tested, to have another man tell her what to do. She's looking forward to the opportunity to show off her talents. She might speak a little French. Or play the pianoforte. She might even take a refreshing turn about the room, to show her figure in the most pleasing light. What color *is* her parachute? And will it match her shoes?

It's the night of my first date with Paul. What an agonizing week it's been. I've lived a whole courtship, relationship, and breakup in a matter of days. I'm exhausted, and the date hasn't even happened yet.

I talked to Walter about the fact that I've been daydreaming constantly about this man and I haven't even met him. I feel fifteen years old. In fact, when I hear Taylor Swift on the radio sing, "When you're fifteen, and someone tells you they love you, you're gonna believe them," I tear up. Not because of the wretched subject-pronoun disagreement in that sentence; I overlook that pet peeve to honor the innocence and trust it holds. No matter our age, we can't stop believing in love. Time and time again we reach for roses, knowing that our hands will bleed. Walter assures me that infatuation happens to everyone, and that I now have a chance to integrate the parts of me that were never expressed. When I was a teenager I didn't act on infatuation. I felt pressured to do everything right, to take care of my mother and my sister. Now I feel I'm about to jump off a cliff into the unknown, and I'm excited and terrified by what I may discover. I realize that my fear is not in meeting Paul, but in meeting myself.

I take a cab to the downtown neighborhood of Streeterville, to a sushi restaurant near Paul's apartment. I find him in the back, facing the wall. I take the seat across from him and get my first look at what is a beautiful smile in a very handsome face. I'm momentarily flustered but Paul orders me a drink and we settle into easy conversation. It occurs to me that my limbo-like state of being not-quite-single is possibly a secret power I didn't know I had. I'm both completely free and yet severely limited by my circumstances. I have nowhere to be but in the moment.

What I learn about the moment is that it has no allegiance to anything that has come before. In one breath Paul offers divorce advice, as if I'm meeting with Paul the accountant, and in the next he's smiling and telling me that I'm beautiful. I struggle to keep up and wish I had been better educated in dating when I was younger. My two most memorable dates in high school involved embarrassing assumptions that my date would be paying for me. In one, at a restaurant before a formal dance, my date forgot his wallet. Since I had no money, I had to wait at the table while he drove home to get it. In another, a different boy invited me to a movie. He walked in before me and paid for himself, then turned and, seeing the panicked look on my face, realized I couldn't buy my own ticket. That time I was the one who had to leave. Twenty-five years later, I've made sure that I have my own cash, but Paul is generous and nonchalant about the bill, and I accept this trait with pleasure, like I'm accepting a refreshing after-dinner mint presented on a plate. There's not the sense there often was with Dave that this time and money could have been better spent elsewhere.

I decide that my currency is my willingness to get back in the game. Now that I've cleared the first-date hurdle, I can breathe easier. Paul seems to present himself as a kind of helpmate, with a gentle been-there-done-that approach, and this makes me assume that he's categorized us as friends. I adjust my expectations, because, resolve or not, in that moment I find that I *have* expectations. Likely they were there all along, soft and close to my heart like the silk of the camisole under my new blouse, meant to be felt rather than seen.

But perhaps Paul does see. After the waiter returns his credit card, he swings himself to my side of the table so he's sitting beside me on the banquet. He leans in and says conspiratorially, "Whether we're going to have a relationship or just be friends. . . ." The rest of the sentence doesn't even register. I'm too startled by this kind of candor. He seems to be saying that whatever the outcome, it will be okay. Maybe it's the two drinks I've had; I feel loose and untethered, free to have choices.

When it's time to leave, Paul asks the busboy to bring over his wheelchair, which has been parked by the coat rack. It's an electric, deluxe model. The busboy turns it on and steers it in jerks and veers to our table. As Paul pulls himself into it I notice two disparate things at once: he wears very nice shoes, and fatigue is beginning to show on his face. I realize the effort he's put into making this date look easy; the thought sobers me. I follow as he snakes his way between tables toward the exit. Some diners look at us, some don't. Some smile and shift their chairs to make more room. I expect to feel more self-conscious in the presence of his wheelchair, but mostly I feel relieved and a little delighted with myself. On the sidewalk we say goodbye, and Paul promises to call.

The next day I tell Abigail that I think I'll see Paul again. In a confession that embarrasses me, I say that all I want is one perfect princess kiss. It's the truth, but not the whole truth. I want so much more. I long to be enveloped in someone's arms and held close to another beating heart. How it would sustain me! And how it would break me, too. I ache with loneliness. One touch and I'll come undone. Even if I continue dating, I can't see my loneliness shifting any time soon. I'll never know anyone as well as I've known Dave over the last twenty years.

Except I didn't know Dave, did I? Maybe the belief that intimacy requires a ladder of years and layer upon layer of moments isn't true. Over the next few days Paul and I talk on the phone a total of three hours. It's more than I've talked to Dave in a long time, and I'm stunned at the connection that can be forged over the nothingness of a phone line. I tell myself that it can't be real, but these days I don't know what *is* real. I'm trying to get to the other side of a raging river, and I can only leap from stone to stone: the photo Paul had on his profile that I can't get out of my mind, clearer to me even than the flesh and blood version from the restaurant; the compliments he gave me; his listening ear and patient presence that make me feel that I'm worth getting to know—each is a step toward safe and solid ground.

We arrange a second date, two weeks later, at the Lookingglass Theatre on Michigan Avenue, to see a production of *Our Town* directed by TV actor and Chicago native David Schwimmer. Because of Paul's wheelchair, we're directed to an elevator that will take us to a different entrance. We must have punched the wrong number because the elevator doors open to an empty hallway. Confused, we venture forward, hearing a man's voice that sounds immediately familiar. It's coming from a large empty room to our left. We peek around the corner to see David Schwimmer, alone, talking on a cell phone. He interrupts his call and comes over to ask if he can help us. He's warm and friendly and tells us to enjoy the show. As we find our way back upstairs to our seats, which are in the front row, thanks to Paul's chair, there's a sense of the magical between us.

The play transports us to the fictional town of Grover's Corners, where life unfolds in ordinary ways. Then comes the third act, bringing tragedy, and the character Emily speaks from beyond the grave, "Just for a moment now we're all together. Mama, just for a moment we're happy. *Let's look at one another.*"

My heart swells and I don't dare to look at Paul. Maybe it's only me who finds this unbearably beautiful.

"I can't go on," Emily says. "It goes so fast. We don't have time to look at one another. I didn't realize . . . Oh, earth, you are too wonderful for anybody to realize you. Do any human beings ever realize life while they live it—every, every minute?"

I vow to realize every minute, painful or glorious, and, as if in response to my thought, Paul raises a hand and scratches his cheek. The sound his hand makes against the stubble on his face is as loud in my ear as the voices from the stage; it makes every fiber in me jump to attention. I feel tuned into him, the *presence* of him, in a way I've never been to anyone.

"They don't understand, do they?" Emily says, and the play ends.

I take these words with me as Paul and I cross Michigan Avenue, settle at a cozy table for dinner and wine, and look at one another. I don't understand why I'm drawn to this person. I don't understand how this can go anywhere, considering the obvious limitations. And I don't understand how, just for this moment, I'm happy. After dinner, Paul escorts me to the parking garage, where I stand beside my car as we say our goodbyes. He takes my hand, pulls me toward him, and kisses me. It may not be the perfect princess kiss; in fact, expecting a woman in her forties to have a romantic moment under the glare of fluorescent lights was a bold move, but I'm glad he made it. And he earned points for wearing nice shoes.

When I share the details of our date with Walter at my next session, he takes a metaphysical view. He suggests that Paul and I are making something unique happen, that there is another realm we are experiencing, beyond expectations, where there are no coincidences, no "wrong floors." After all, *Our Town* is about the beauty and transience of each moment. He advises me to let go of planning and worrying and to just be present, to be more direct in response to Paul's directness. But what if I'm too enthusiastic and my feelings change? I ask. What if I hurt him? Walter says to let Paul in on my thoughts and trust him to take care of himself. He reminds me that I have no practice doing this, and that I don't know what a grownup relationship looks like.

I interject, thinking that Walter is missing the same thing I'm missing, "He's in a wheelchair. He has a serious disability. Maybe I'm just swayed by his good looks and flattery. I'm not being practical."

"Everyone has something to deal with," Walter says. "Someone like Dave keeps it inside where no one can see it. Paul can't hide. He's forced to be vulnerable."

Is this what's appealing to me? Paul is a mix of bravery and brokenness that I've never seen, and it pulls at my heart. Author Brene Brown writes that being vulnerable is not weakness, that it's courage beyond measure. It's daring greatly. Do I dare to let Paul in? Is it possible that my own brokenness could be lovable? Something Paul said during dinner comes back to me. It was the same thing Walter said, only Paul called it his "box of rocks." We all have our own "box of rocks." For the first time, I want to look closer and, because of Paul, the rocks are looking more and more like jewels.

Cue the orchestra, because this is where I step into my own magic kingdom. I feel as if I've taken a potion. In equal parts I am humbled, inspired, grateful, flattered, revived. But the final ingredient, the one Paul adds in a generous dose and that proves more powerful than pixie dust, is appreciation. He thanks me for everything—big things, like my kindness, generosity, compassion, and little things, like refilling his glass or not flinching if he stumbles—and I'm drunk on it. Everything softens; it's as though someone has smeared Vaseline on the lens of my life. Maybe it's that I refuse to be left behind. If Dave and the kids are going to Disney World, I'm going to La-La Land. And I'm going with Paul.

We've had three dates and spent hours on the phone when spring break arrives, my family leaves, and I'm left alone in the house. I invite Paul to dinner, eager for him to see where and how I live. The night is snowy and cold. He takes a taxi over. He's able to get from the taxi to my front stairs using a cane, and by putting my arm around his waist I'm able to help him climb the steps to the door. I'm touched at the way he lets me do this, and at the courage it must require. I wish I could acknowledge these things, but I don't know how. I squeeze his arm as I guide him to my sofa and help him take off his coat. He pulls a smashed bouquet of flowers from his backpack. We eat Thai food and watch a sappy Nicholas Sparks movie.

As the night progresses, the weather worsens, and it's easy to see that he'll have a treacherous time getting home. Even getting around my apartment, using his cane and hugging the wall, the banister, or my arm, becomes more difficult as he gets tired. He'll stay the night, we decide, and though I let him share my bed, he climbs in fully clothed, joking about keeping one foot on the floor. This is a reasonable plan, I think. I feel good. We lie beside each other looking at the ceiling in comfortable, companionable silence.

Then, without warning, I see Dave standing at the foot of the bed, as real as he was on a recent night when he barged in and woke me, wanting to talk. I will this specter to leave, *just leave me be*, but he won't go. Shame rises in me, as if I've been caught cheating. I begin to cry, silently at first, horrified at what is now the weirdest, least-sexy date on record.

Paul reaches for my hand. "Sweetie, tell me what you're feeling."

Tell me what you're feeling? Did he really just say that? He might have said "Rapunzel, let down your golden hair." Or "Juliet, Juliet, wherefore art thou Juliet?" That's how magical, how *epic,* this question is to me. It's the stuff of fairy tales, not real life as I've known it.

Call me crazy—or delusional, desperate, immature. Call me done for, because with those six words I know: I'm in love.

14 Blown Apart

Something elemental changes in me after my night with Paul. I feel emotional and miserable. All frivolity is gone, and in its place is what I can only imagine is lovesickness. Its symptoms include an inevitability and sense of responsibility that feels crushing. At the same time it's the closest thing to freedom I've ever known. If this isn't love, I don't know what is. But which is the imposter, the heart I carried for twenty years, or this resurrected, unpredictable one?

My next date with Paul is at his apartment. He lives on the twenty-ninth floor of a high-rise with a spectacular view of the Chicago skyline and Lake Michigan. He's put a lot of work into creating an indoor picnic for us. There's a blanket on the living room floor, candles on the coffee table, and a dinner of wine, sushi, and chocolate cake. I'm impressed, though I have a hard time knowing what to say. Chitchat seems superficial, yet my true feelings are unfamiliar and ungainly; they encroach on me like a stranger who insists on standing too close.

This wasn't supposed to happen. I wanted dating to be fun. In my last session with Walter, I told him that I never intended to tell my dates about myself or my situation. I wanted to be sassy and *au courant*; no one had to know what was happening inside. Walter said, "You didn't pick someone like that. You emailed a real person."

I feel far from real in the next weeks. The lovesickness works its way into my bones. One day I'm up, the next I'm down. Paul helps, or doesn't help, by sending texts that couldn't be more perfect:

> *To say I think about you every hour would be an*
> *understatement.*
> *I find you intriguing.*

And this sweet syllabic verse:

> *Wow. Coma sleep.*
> *Dreams of Tammy.*
> *Smile on my face.*

He calls me every morning, greeting me with, "Hello, beautiful," and those words lift and ease me into my days. Our daily talks uncover connections that seem downright spooky. In addition to attending the same college, we discover that our dorms were next to each other, our first jobs in Chicago were in neighboring high-rise buildings, our middle children were born one day apart, and most uncannily, that our spouses share the same divorce attorney. In a city the size of Chicago, what are the odds of this? Because of this bizarre lawyer connection, Paul is not unlike a quarterback who has memorized the playbook. He knows the game, he knows which passes will be thrown, and when Dave's side is throwing a Hail Mary. When I tell Paul about the court order I received requiring me to see a vocational expert, he nods knowingly.

"I've seen how Dave's attorney works, and you'll be put through the paces," he says. "All of this is to run up the clock. Let it play out. Be patient and nothing will come of it."

Paul's divorce was finalized less than two years before we met and was far from amicable, so I'm surprised when he offers to come to the courthouse with me when my next court date comes around. I would think he would want to stay as far away from the Daley Center as possible. But he makes it seem as if it's no big deal for him since he lives downtown. I'm not fooled. Even though he's adept at riding the city buses in his wheelchair, I know getting anywhere on his own is never "no big deal." I gratefully accept, telling him that he can wait in the cafe across the street. Meanwhile, I take the elevator up to the windowless, anxiety-filled room where a stone-faced bailiff watches everyone's every move, and I'm calmed just knowing Paul is close by.

I begin to have what I would call otherworldly thoughts, like is it possible that Paul is an angel? I mean a *real* one. One day, after reading a chapter in one of Sonia Choquette's books about how angels live among us, I leave a cafe and pass an old man on the sidewalk who locks eyes with me. His gaze is laser sharp and somehow *knowing*. It jolts through me along with the thought: He's an angel. I keep walking and then I can't help myself—I stop and look back. The man has also stopped and is looking back at me, a small smile on his lips. Unnerved, I hurry home, telling myself I made up that bizarre, electrically charged moment, but knowing that I didn't.

It's with the same sense of divine synchronicity that I think of Paul and entertain the idea that he was dropped into my life for the sole purpose of softening my broken, brittle heart. My imagination, always untamable, grows even wilder. Will I discover someday that he's only been in my mind? When I relive our moments together, will I realize that no one but me has ever seen him? It's preposterous, but that's how private and preordained our time together seems. I'm in another world. I wander grocery aisles, unable to focus, arriving home one night with peanut butter but no bread, two apples, cereal, half-and-half instead of milk, and a bottle of red wine when I wanted white. After a therapy session, I walk six blocks looking for my car before remembering that I moved it to a parking lot next to Walter's office.

The shrillness of the school bell brings me back every morning. I still have to be a mom and carry on, but I no longer want to chat with the other moms. I feel too divided, both from them and within myself. I'm simultaneously sheepish and belligerent, broken and shiny new, lonely and standoffish. Anyway, when did they all become friends? I feel like I missed a memo, and a door has closed. Growing up as the perennial new girl in school, I learned that you can't just barge into a group of girls. You have to start with one and let her be an opening to the rest. But I'm too old and self-conscious to play girl games. I go to Jed's parent-teacher conference alone and spend the whole time wondering how to tell the teacher that Jed's father and I are divorcing. I want to use the words *sudden divorce* like some kind of code, so she'll know . . . what? That I'm the parent to be trusted? When I do manage to tell her, my cheeks hot and red, she reacts as if she already knows. Of *course* she knows. Like the Paul Simon song says, "Losing love is like a window in your heart. Everyone sees you're blown apart."

Last summer I saw an old friend of mine at Logan's baseball game. She was different. Instead of a demure sundress and cardigan, she wore faded blue jeans, a white tank top, tousled long hair, and cowboy boots. She looked dressed for a NASCAR race, not mom duty. She told me that she was going to the Gwen Stefani concert with a girlfriend. That night I had a vague and unsettling dream about her, and the next day I opened my door to find her husband standing there. He was also an old friend, and when I saw his face I knew immediately what he was about to say. She was leaving him. Were there signs? Had he noticed her new/old blue jeans? Had he seen the prefabricated tear in the knee and known it represented a tear in the fabric of their marriage? In what ways had Dave worn his unhappiness? There had been no new clothes, no facial hair, no gadgets or newfound friends. And yet I should have spotted something. If I could dream the truth about a friend, why couldn't I recognize the dream state that was my life? And if I saw incongruence in my friend, certainly the moms in the schoolyard see it in me as well. Do they know that I am *dating* someone? And what if my preoccupation with Paul is blinding me to my kids' needs? I make a mental note to start taking all three of them to therapy and involve myself more in their school activities. Soon after, Jed's class puts on a presentation called "We the People." It starts with the kids leading the parents in small groups through the hallways on a scavenger hunt that involves answering history questions. What year did Columbus discover America? What is the significance of the Emancipation Proclamation? I attempt to focus on these events as a way to gain perspective on my life. No one will one day remember that on a December day in the twenty-first century, Dave devastated his former ally, colonized their home, or vanquished a joint checking account. My circumstances are insignificant, and I wish the victim in me would get with the program.

The presentation ends in the gym, and as the class takes the stage, I find a seat in the back where I can quickly scan the room and confirm that Dave is not there. I barely have time to read the program when, to my complete shock and delight, Jed steps to the microphone and begins singing *It's a Grand Old Flag*. I've never heard him sing, and he never mentioned that he had a solo performance. This is certainly evidence of my neglect, but before I can indulge my feelings of incompetence, the drama club files onto the risers and an orchestral version of *Under Pressure* begins. I recognize it as a song by the band Queen because Dave is big fan; when I was pregnant with Logan, he suggested in all seriousness that we name him Mercury in honor of Freddy Mercury. I watch as, one by one, dressed all in white, children dance and spin across the stage, moving expressively, each one seemingly unafraid and free from the terror of knowing what this world is about. Tears sting my eyes as I hear the song lyric in my head: this is our last dance.

Afterwards, like so many afternoons, I hide in my minivan, holding myself together until I can get to Paul. His room is like a tower in a faraway land. I escape there, to the glittering lights of the city, where I try to see beyond, to a brighter light, a broader view. With Paul I feel so happy, then suddenly I sway under a gust of despair. I miss Dave. Eventually this lovesickness will wear off and I'll want my best friend. Won't I?

15 The Party's Over

More and more, we are a house divided. Dave sleeps in the basement and uses the downstairs bathroom, and the kids and I stay mostly upstairs. We pass in the kitchen, and I come to dread the way he plunks himself down at the table in the mornings and noisily digs into his Special K, as if it were the most normal thing in the world to be sharing this space. I don't want to share anything. I didn't want to share my husband. I don't want to share my career plans with a stranger, or my spending habits with a lawyer, or my children with the babe-of-the-week. I can't stand living with this stranger. I want him out, and yet I'm frozen, unable to make it happen because I'm terrified of living alone and caring for the kids by myself.

I'm also jumpy and paranoid. Ever since Dave saw my emails with Scott, I don't know where I can safely leave my computer. And what about my journal? I'm tired of hiding it, and I'm running out of hiding places. I find myself peering suspiciously into my closet, certain Dave has been in there. I hid some of the kids' baby pictures under my sweaters. They're still there, but he could find and take them at any time.

"Can you promise you'll stay out of my room?" I ask.

"I won't go in unless I need to."

But I've learned to decode his sentences. "I'd like a firm yes or no, please."

"I don't plan on going in."

"Can you *please* give me a direct answer?"

"Okay. I promise." He leaves the room, but immediately comes back. "You know what? I don't promise. It's my house."

"Why do you have to be like that? Remember what happened last time you went in the bedroom, while we were in Tennessee."

"What?"

Has he really forgotten that I slapped his face? I shake my head and turn away.

"I'm not going to go in there," he says. "I'm just messing with you."

But he does keep coming in, usually after I've gone to bed. Several times he wakes me with questions about bird-nesting, or switching parenting nights, or school events—always things that Dave would argue are reasonable, yet the timing is invasive and unnerves me. I decide to have locks put on both the bedroom and office doors.

It's Saturday, the day after Jed's birthday party. He had a few boys over, and Dave led them in a Nerf gun war. Stale cake litters the dining room table, streamers sag from the chandelier, and the balloons that cover the floor slowly, sadly exhale. Before I tackle the clean-up, I call a locksmith who says he can come right away. Perfect. It's officially my day with the kids. They're entrenched in the basement in front of the TV, and Dave is out.

Soon after, I hear someone at the front door and assume it's the locksmith. It's Dave, back from wherever he was. He doesn't tell me his schedule and I don't ask. I wish today I had. There's a knot in my stomach as I watch him putter around and then, thankfully, he goes into the bathroom. I hear the shower turn on just as the locksmith arrives.

He's a pleasant, older Hispanic man with a broad smiling face. I lead him to the office and watch him make fast work of installing a deadbolt. I breathe a little easier. I have every right to do this. This is my house too. He hands me two keys to the new office door lock and we head for the bedroom. He's drilling a hole in the wood door when Dave appears.

"What's going on?" Dave asks.

"Nothing that concerns you."

Dave assesses the situation. His faces reads *I'm so reasonable*, but I recognize his quiet outrage, a mask of friendliness over hard bones of fury. It will stay in place while an invisible rubber mallet comes out swinging. Not a sharp or heavy tool, the mallet's job is to wear me down while appearing harmless.

"What work have you done?" he asks the locksmith, who is beginning to look uncomfortable.

"I had him put a deadbolt on my office," I say.

Dave addresses the locksmith. "I need one of those keys."

I step forward, turning my body away from the poor man so he doesn't have to hear. "Dave, please!" I hate that my voice is unsteady. "I just found out that the person I thought I knew is a complete stranger to me, that I've been lied to for years, and nothing is as I thought. My whole world is broken, and I would like these two rooms to be a safe place for me."

Dave ignores this. "Please make me a key to these locks."

The locksmith blinks, looking from me to Dave to me again. Why does this man have to be so kindly looking, so fatherly? He's the type I always want to impress (that's a whole other session with Walter), and this only multiplies my embarrassment.

"He gave me two keys. Leave him alone and let him finish."

Dave has positioned himself between us and seems to be taking up more space than me and the small Hispanic man combined.

Appearances be damned. "I'm trying to keep him out," I explain, willing myself to stand taller and speak forcefully. Locksmiths must hear this all the time. And worse. The man doesn't make a move, so we all stand there awkwardly.

Dave throws up his hands. "I guess I have to call the police."

"Go ahead." I motion for the locksmith to continue and walk away. Dave follows.

"Tammy, let's not play this game. I have a right to those keys!"

I sit on the sofa, pressing my shaking knees together, while Dave makes the call. He speaks calmly, asking for a squad car, then stands by the window, waiting. The scene is as surreal and frozen as a Salvatore Dali painting, disturbed (or enhanced?) only when the locksmith shuffles in, his feet parting a sea of birthday balloons. He lays the keys diplomatically on the coffee table.

"Party's over, huh?" His brown eyes are liquid soft.

"Yeah." I hand him his check. "Party's over."

I never would have believed that in this short span of time I would be forced to think about escorts, send a desperate text to my husband's lover, or find myself on my front porch telling two police officers why I need to lock my husband out. Any one of those scenarios would be, in my opinion, better suited to the Jerry Springer show. Yet here I am, in broad daylight, red-faced and wishing we would please step inside, praying the police leave before the kids notice them. After Dave explains the key "emergency," they ask me if he has assaulted me. No. Am I in imminent danger? No. *But* . . . I motion one of them over with my head and we cram into the tiny foyer together.

"He comes into my room in the middle of the night," I whisper. "And I don't know what he's going to do because he's been so unpredictable lately."

"I'm sorry," he says, "but he has to have the keys. It's his house." He suggests I keep a cell phone next to my bed.

"I'm only asking for two rooms to myself!" But he can only shrug. He steps back outside where his partner is talking to Dave and then they leave, giving Dave no more than a stern look. I want to shout at them *to serve and protect? Really?* but I shrink back meekly. They have better things to do, and I feel like a fool for what I've done. Any bruises I may have are on the inside, and everyone knows those don't count.

16 Stayin' Alive

My eyes are closed and I pretend to sleep, but there is no rest for the wicked, sayeth the Lord; I must be very wicked. Jed comes in at 5:30 a.m. and lies down beside me. I open my eyes and we stare at each other, our faces inches apart.

"Mom, are you still mad at Dad?"

I don't know what to say, but his big brown eyes await an answer.

"It's not really that we're mad at each other," I say slowly, "so much as we need time apart. We email each other right now when we need to talk."

"If you're in the same house, why don't you just talk?"

I blink. I've got nothing.

"How long will you be mad?"

Deep breath. "Daddy is having some problems that he needs to work out, and we're going to be patient and give him space, okay?"

Surprisingly, he's satisfied. He rolls over, presses his back into my stomach, and falls asleep. An hour later Logan comes in to tell me he's had a nightmare.

"Dad sold the house without telling us," he says. "There was a store in our house, and Dad was working there, but then the police came in and fired him."

Did Logan see the police? He couldn't have. And what's this about

Dave selling the house? I won't allow this vision to come true. I know that ghostly fears are clinging to the kids' psyches like lint clings to wet clothes. I have my own childhood memories, brightly colored despite years of wearing, washing, and folding them into shape: my mother, pregnant with my younger sister, is in hysterics after discovering my father's affair. A man from the church comes. He speaks in hushed tones. I hear him say the words "hissy fit" and for years, well into my teens, I think that a hissy fit is a medical condition. My father's other woman is his secretary. My mother breaks into the woman's home and throws dirt on her bed. This I learn much later, but the image inserts itself here, taking its rightful place in the story and in my memory bank. Time stretches like that, snapping events into place or breaking at the weak points, depending on the tension.

Another memory without a timestamp: we are driving with my mom when she sees my father's car at the A&W restaurant. She pulls into the parking lot. I'm excited, hoping for a root beer float. Inside, my father is sitting with a woman. She has long dark hair. My mom directs us to a booth in the corner, and she goes to sit beside him. Something is very wrong. There is sadness and silence thickening the air. We leave without ordering. Eventually we all move to a different city to leave the sadness behind, but it follows and becomes sharper, settling as acid in our stomachs. I go a whole summer without eating more than a few bites. My father comes home drunk and vomits in the driveway, leaning out the car door while an 8-track tape plays the Bee Gees: *Well, you can tell by the way I use my walk, I'm a woman's man, no time to talk.*

I have become my mother. A slight exaggeration, perhaps. I do have a college degree. My mother didn't know how to write a check when my parents divorced. She had never handled her own money. At least

I understand our budget. I enter my expenses into Quickbooks. I know how to run reports and read our tax returns. But it's been years since I earned money as a freelance copywriter. I may be a new generation of *smart women* but I still worry. Is Dave going to take care of me and the kids? What if he completely flakes out? What if he quits his job?

The helplessness, the sense of doom, that my mother must have felt flares in me and I understand it in a way I never could before. I was sixteen when my dad moved out. We'd been in Ohio less than a year, uprooted yet again, this time to a whole new state. It might have been a different country; acclimating was, for me, that difficult. As my parents' divorce went on, things became stranger. My dad turned off the heat and the hot water and stopped buying groceries. My siblings and I ate toast after school because that was all there was, and I remember begging my older brother Bryan, who was a year older and had a car, to take me to McDonald's with him where, for thirty-five cents scrounged from my dad's pants, I could get a hamburger.

It was a time of small hurtful things and grand vengeful gestures: no food one day, the next day a silent meal prepared by my dad, after which he'd read us confusing passages from the Bible; a fight over a crystal punch bowl that had not been used in fifteen years; arguments about where my younger brother would live—a campaign to help him "decide" that ended with him choosing my dad; the appearance of a new emerald-green sports car in the driveway, while, inside, household items were being stockpiled or spirited away.

Bryan's misery was so great that he became legally emancipated at seventeen and moved back to Michigan to live alone. It was the single greatest loss of my adolescent life, but I don't recall allowing myself to feel it. I had my own way of coping. Each morning I would vomit, the sound of the approaching yellow bus acting like a Pavlovian bell, triggering a release that allowed me to empty myself enough to ease into the normalcy of school.

Finally a new normal evolved for my mom, my sister, and me. With both my brothers gone, it was just the three of us, and we eventually moved to a tiny apartment in the back corner of a large complex. Our windows looked out on a parking lot and a chain-link fence, but there was a pool and a playground for my little sister. I missed my brothers, but I was glad to be away from my dad. I threw myself into my junior year, playing flute and twirling baton for the marching band, joining powder puff football, crying when a boy I dated dumped me because I stopped him from feeling me up at a party. I lay on the sofa crying and nauseated for two days, wondering what was wrong with me that such a popular boy, captain of the swim team, could have smiled at me and kissed me the way he had, then sighed and turned away, letting me know instantly and unequivocally that I was a waste of time.

Years later, I'm back on a sofa. I feel the city shakin' and everybody breakin'. Decades collapse again in a blip, but the same thought lives on: What could I have done differently?

That night Dave and I talk for a long time, and I'm struck again by the way he speaks without saying anything. He wants us to be friendly. He wishes I would *cooperate*—a word I feel compelled to look up, which means *working toward the same end*. He says he cares about me and hates to see me suffer. I begin to understand that, by Dave's logic, I will stop suffering if I agree to his terms. He'll take nothing less than fifty-fifty residential custody, even though he works full-time and travels, even though I have been a full-time mom for ten years. He entreats me again to be *reasonable*. He must know that this is my kryptonite. More than anything, I want to be seen by the world, Dave included, as reasonable, deserving, *good*. I have assigned myself the role of saint. With embarrassment I recall my speech to him, a few days after he delivered his news, when I took the stage determined to be the best "Marriage Reconstruction" teacher the world had ever seen. We sat in our bedroom and I said, "Happiness is inside of you. You've got to stop looking outside yourself." As if he would go, "Wow! You're right. I never considered that!" All the while the angular woman in the framed Modigliani painting over our bed gazed down with her world-weary look that said, "Oh, Tammy, Tammy, Tammy." She's seen it all—the folly and fragility of human relationships and the futility of one person thinking she can change another. Her stare is as stark and inescapable as the words of poetry that are carved into the mantle above the fireplace at the Lakeside Inn, words that hovered over our shoulders as Dave and I exchanged wedding vows: *Time passes. Art alone endures.*

There are two definitions for the word endure: 1. To suffer patiently. 2. To remain in existence. One sounds miserable, the other strong and noble. Which do I choose? The question becomes not what could I have done differently, but what can I do differently now?

When I see an apartment for rent several blocks away, I drag Dave to go see it. The two of us walk over, and his bored indifference infuriates me. I point out amenities as if there is an HGTV camera pointed at me, trying to cover my growing embarrassment over the fact that we are obviously wasting the landlord's time.

Back outside, I explode. "What's wrong with you? You need to find an apartment! Don't you want to get settled somewhere now, so the kids can adjust to it over the summer?"

He shrugs and I feel like a mother arguing with a teenager. Why am I involved in this process at all? This is so clearly not my business. Whatever role I must grow into, there are certain aspects that have to be left behind, beginning with Dave's *mother* and *secretary*.

"I'm not moving out until we have the visitation schedule decided," he says.

I want to throttle him. "What's the big mystery? Do you really think your schedule will be much different than every other divorced dad out there?"

He doesn't answer but his look says it all. Yes. Yes, he does.

Later he says, "I have an idea. Maybe you could get a job at a hotel and get one of the rooms as part of your pay. Then we could each use it while the other is with the kids."

"How about *you* do that?" I shoot back. "You have more experience with hotels than I do!"

I may not be able to rush Dave out of the house, but I can hasten our separation in another way. Our Honda Odyssey van is leased in his name and, as much as I love it, and especially the heated seats, it's time for me to get my own car. Now that we have a temporary support order in effect, I can show that I have some income. In fact, I learn from the salesman at CarMax that a court order can be considered more reliable than a pay stub. As he shows me around the lot, I realize that the first and last time I bought a car was my senior year in high school when I saved $800 from my Bob Evans waitress job and got a 1971 Dodge Dart. The idea of choosing my own car again now gives me a small thrill. I take my time perusing my options before settling on a 1996 royal blue Ford SUV. It's sporty but not unwieldy, bright but not overly flashy like that green sports car my dad brought home during my parents' divorce. Mostly I can't resist the name of this particular model: it's an Escape. I'll take it.

17 A Journey of 2,500 Miles

Dave seems shocked to see me with my own Escape. He watches me switch April's booster seat from the van to my Ford with a wary look on his face, as if he's thinking of telling me to take it back. I'm baffled by the way these uncoupling necessities baffle him. Has he forgotten that he proclaimed his extramarital activities to me like he was delivering a decree? Then he handed down his decisions with no more negotiation than a monarch shouting, "Off with her head!" I can't forget that he said he wanted to "wrap things up" with me in four weeks. I imagine him literally wrapping me in plastic, freezing me in place. Is that what he wanted? Did it ever occur to him that I would go on living, separate from him?

I have the disoriented sense of being ousted, then chained; silenced, then told to explain myself. But I have to continue disentangling myself from him. The car is a start. Now, with those keys in hand, I set out to unlock other practical matters, like where will I live? Is it possible for me to keep the house? Looking back, I realize with a sinking feeling that I was the one who pushed us into our first condominium, arguing that we needed to get a foot in the real estate market if we ever wanted to trade up to a house in a decent neighborhood. Dave would likely have been content to stay in our third floor two-bedroom rental apartment. I did all the legwork for that first property and again for our house. Dave wasn't even with me the first time I looked at our house with the real estate agent. He wasn't there all the times I waited in the demolished, unheated first floor in the January cold with our month-old daughter to show prospective tenants the upstairs rental unit. I was stunned by the number of people who made appointments to see the place—sometimes just thirty minutes in advance, saying they were in the neighborhood, could they please just pop in?—and then didn't come. I'd spend the time mentally decorating while I covered April's tiny face, afraid that she would inhale the sawdust covering the freshly sanded hardwood floors. And when the remodeling began, I made the visits to talk with the contractor about carpet samples, paint chips, and recessed lighting. It wasn't that Dave was disinterested; he was busy working. That's what I believed.

I also believed that he was devoted to me and me alone, only to hear him say he was never passionately in love with me and doesn't believe in monogamy. He never shared those feelings with me—that I know with every fiber of my being. But it's possible that he said he didn't want to buy a house. It's possible that he had to be talked into having a third child. It's possible that I took charge when it came to my vision of our family and home. This seemed natural; I'm the visionary, the global thinker, the hearth-keeper. I'm the woman, and I still believe that the feminine power lies in guiding the ship by scanning the horizon and consulting the stars, while the masculine energy powers the engines and protects the vessel. I thought Dave and I were working together. Was I so wrong?

When Valentine's Day came the year we bought the house, Dave surprised me by taking me there for our date. We were still living in the condo while the renovations were underway. The electricity was finally on, and he had strung lights around the dining room and set up several TV trays for our dinner of Italian takeout and red wine. As we sat in the dusty, unfinished room in the dim, dancing candlelight,

I could see a lifetime of years flickering on the walls: our children laughing and hiding in the deep narrow Victorian closets; the built-in oak hutch stocked with serving dishes and wine glasses I'd bring out for family dinners; countless nights of homework at a long farmhouse table; teenagers throwing a Nerf basketball around the basement; me, an old woman in a sunhat, watching my garden every year for the perennials to return to me like faithful friends. I saw all of this in an instant and a bubble of joy rose in me. "We're going to be so happy here!" I exclaimed and was immediately, inexplicably embarrassed. I recall covering my mouth as if I'd belched and feeling sheepish about my giddiness. Bursts of unbridled happiness were not common between Dave and me. We were clever, we made jokes, we laughed, but always we were anchored by our serious, hard-working genes. In that moment, I felt silly and free, yet somehow instinctively knew that I should rein it in.

It's been several years since that Valentine's Day. The oak cabinet I hauled in from the alley and painted is now chipped on one side. The sofa where I dozed the night Dave called me to the table has a stain on one cushion from April's crushed "boo-berries." The dining room table is not the farmhouse type I desired. It's a flea market find with scratches and one wobbly leg. Overall the look is no longer as polished as it was the day the decorators left. Yet I loved where I'd landed, and Dave was part of that landscape. Whether it was actually him or my idea of him that occupied a place, I don't know. I couldn't separate one from the other.

But now we'll have to separate all of this, deciding who gets the sofa or the cabinet, or where the table will go on wobbling. We'll have to divide dishes and dismantle beds and deconstruct photo albums, leaving stark white squares under yellow-edged pages as reminders that those memories have been taken away. Then will come the heavy lifting—separating dreams from reality, past from present, blows from blessings. I'll have to see myself as someone separate in order to decide what I want.

I sit at my table and consider the four walls around me. I look at the floor where I slid to my knees. This house holds pain now and I should get out, start fresh. It's old and creaky and not too attractive. The front porch is sagging a bit, and the white siding looks dull and sad. The dirt in the side yard turned out to be mostly gray clay that hides decades of decay; I've unearthed shards of glass, old bottle tops, bits of plastic, even spark plugs. Countless bags of topsoil haven't been able to infuse the necessary nutrients down deep, where it counts, and only the most stubborn plants—the self-propagating daylilies—have survived.

But in the words of Jane Austen, "One does not love a place the less for having suffered in it, unless it has been all suffering, nothing but suffering." This house has stood here for more than a hundred years, and I don't want to abandon it because it's known pain. It's kept me safe and dry and (mostly) warm. One day it goes a step further and delivers a gift to me. I answer a knock at the door to find a man with a clipboard. He explains that he works for a service that files appeals for property tax refunds. Apparently Chicago homeowners can be overtaxed, and most never know that they can request a review and reimbursement of overpayment. He says that if I simply sign his form, I will likely get a check, minus a percentage that his company will keep.

"Don't you need both homeowners to sign?" I ask, but he says no. So I sign, figuring I have nothing to lose. I don't tell Dave about it, and I soon forget about it altogether. Then I open the mail one day to find a check for seven hundred dollars made out to me. I don't tell Dave about this either. Instead I thank the house. It's as if we have a secret understanding. *I've got your back,* the house says to me, and I vow to return the favor.

꧁

Soon school lets out and, without the school bell to mark my days, I sink into a limbo-like state. Nearly five months have gone by since I filed the divorce petition, and having Dave in the basement is increasingly difficult. He's said nothing about looking at more apartments and seems as content to sleep on a lumpy sofa as he was to use cinder blocks and plywood in lieu of bookshelves when we first moved in together. I can't understand this any more than I understood that. All I know is that, even though Dave is the one effectively chained to the basement, I'm the one who feels like a hostage. So I beg my attorney Scott to do something about our living arrangements and he promises that he'll talk to the judge at our next court date, still nearly a month away.

As Paul warned, the court process is tortuously slow. Matters that seem clear-cut devolve into minutia in the hands of attorneys, and a transposed number or missing signature is all it takes to declare a four-week continuance. I'm anxious about legal costs. When I express my concerns to Scott he tells me that payment will most likely come from Dave's retirement fund.

"I know you didn't like it when Dave's attorney accused you of charging things frivolously," he says. "But I'm going to tell you to charge your expenses for now. It will all get worked out in the end."

The end. I wonder when that will come. Part of me is desperate for it; another part dreads it. Part of me hates Dave for putting us through this; another part feels sorry for him. It seems that everything has been split down the middle, including me.

So I string my days together the best I can; hours with Paul are the beads that brighten them. In between I hang on to whatever thread of normalcy I can find: a trip to the beach, teaching Jed to ride a bike, reading *The Little Mermaid* to April for the eight-hundredth time, planting flowers in a yard that may soon belong to someone else. I'm no longer taking sleeping pills at night, but anxiety is still clouding my thoughts, so I make an appointment to see Janet, a Healing

Touch practitioner. My doctor first referred me to her years ago, when we were planning my sister Melanie's intervention. She helped me approach that experience with more calmness and clarity, and I need her help now.

When I tell Janet that Dave has refused to move out and about the helplessness I feel, she suggests doing a cord release. She explains that, in our relationships, we form energetic cords between one another, and that these cords can keep us tethered to patterns that no longer serve us.

I lie on the table and close my eyes, relaxing as Janet moves her hands through my aura and talks in a soothing voice. She asks me to tune into my emotions about Dave and notice where I feel them in my body. My hands go immediately to my solar plexus. Janet guides my breathing as she moves to that area.

I begin crying. I have an image of holding a great boulder of grief in my hands. My arms are aching and I want so badly to lay it down. I feel this way with Paul sometimes. I wish I could say, *Can you hold this for me for a while? Just let me hand it to you and I'll pick it up later.* And in his way, with his patience and charm, he does. But in other ways, he can't. His hands are full of his own brokenness, and the request is too big for someone I haven't known long. I'm bereft, and no one, including Paul, can ease this sense I have of losing my best friend.

Janet asks if there is a prayer I've been using.

"Yes. *Be still and know that I am God.*" I repeat this silently to myself as Janet clears away what feels like a weight from my abdomen. At some point a lightness lifts me, and I float, half-dreaming. When the session ends, I tell her that I saw a hummingbird.

"Different animals carry different energies," she says. "There's a book called *Animal Speak* that you may want to explore."

When I look in *Animal Speak*, I read that the hummingbird is a symbol for accomplishing that which seems impossible. She brings a message of tireless joy. She is unique among birds because she can fly backward, forward, and sideways. She has incredible endurance, flying for days and sometimes completing a journey of twenty-five hundred miles, leaving scientists baffled as to how she stores the energy. She is not afraid of any predator, and has been known to chase off eagles. She is fiercely independent and likes to be alone and free. The mothers are hard workers and receive no help from a mate.

That night, I'm in the living room watching TV. The kids are asleep. Dave comes in and stands awkwardly in the middle of the room.

"I was wondering if you want to get frisky," he says.

I hesitate, as if considering. "No thanks. That won't work for me."

He nods agreeably and leaves. It's a strange request, certainly, but even stranger is that I don't think I've ever spoken those words—*that won't work for me.* What's more, I don't feel a maelstrom of emotions. There is no anger, indignation, or sense of obligation, no fear or guilt about rejecting him, no second-guessing my answer or wishing I'd been gentler or kinder. For a split second, I feel detached. For one precious moment, I feel strong. I feel free.

At last we're standing again before the judge, and Scott argues that the current cohabitation situation between Dave and me is not healthy for the kids and is unnecessarily drawing out the process. Dave protests that we haven't signed a visitation agreement yet that will give him the fifty-fifty arrangement he demands.

"You'll get the kids every Wednesday night and every other weekend until you can agree to something else," the judge tells him. Then he orders him to move out by August first and enters a document that gives me possession of the house. Refinancing the mortgage and removing Dave from it will take some time, considering we currently owe more than the house is worth, but for now, it belongs to me. Dave, remarkably, says nothing, but the glower on his face tells me he's furious. Perhaps in exchange for this victory, I let him know later, via email, that I agree to try mediation.

What I don't say is that I have no intention of being reasonable.

Part Two

Give me a wound that only God can heal.

—Source unknown

18 Only God

I'm alone now. Or am I? Dave sublets a three-bedroom apartment from a friend a few miles away. He moves out and Spirit moves in. Or, more accurately, comes close enough that I begin to recognize the feel of it. If only it weren't so fleeting! I strain to hear God's voice over the words of my son Jed when he says, "Dad laughs. You don't."

It's true. I'm not the "fun" parent. I feel dull, unimaginative, and barely able to cope as a single mom. I've managed to hold our everyday lives together, but we need to do more than just survive. So we're embarking on a vacation. Besides our visit to my mom, it's the first time I'll have the kids for a solid week, and I'm scared. I want to show them that the four of us can be a unit. The problem is that I don't really believe it.

I've chosen a YMCA family camp in northern Wisconsin as our destination, reasoning that at least there will be a group there, with a staff and planned activities, to ease my way. It's a six-hour drive from Chicago, and once we're packed into the car, I begin to panic. I spend the first hour trying to regulate my breathing. I tell myself that I can turn back anytime, and when the kids ask me something, I snap at them, "Be quiet! Mom's thinking!"

But instead of waiting for quiet, I turn up the radio. I listen to country singer Randy Travis sing about staying sober, the same

Randy Travis who was arrested the day before, naked and drunk. It's proof that life is day to day. We are never in that happy ending. I don't like this. I thought there would be more of an arrival—some*where* I could lean over and put my hands on my knees and exhale. *Whew! I did it.* Where is that spot? Will I find it on this road to Wisconsin?

I snap off the radio and ask my daughter to sing. She has a beautiful voice and is always happy to serenade us, even over the shouts of her brothers to "please shut up!"

She launches into *Jesus Take the Wheel*. It's been a favorite of ours for some time, but she only recently learned the correct words. When she was three years old she thought the lyrics were "Jesus Take the Wii" and she would put her headphones on and croon this at the top of her lungs, oblivious to the rest of us laughing.

Now here we are, plunging into a week without the Wii, or the iPods, or the phones. All because, in a moment of misplaced enthusiasm, I decided that we could use time away with only each other. What was I thinking? What am I trying to prove, and to whom?

April sings along with Carrie Underwood, "I can't do this on my own. I'm letting go."

But letting go is no laughing matter. It's a tight-fisted, white-knuckle feeling in my stomach, a certainty that if I don't perform all the correct tasks in the correct order, we'll crash and burn. Even when we arrive in Minocqua safe and sound, I remain on edge. This is a family camp, and I immediately note that all the other families look intact and complete. Even our cabin is apart from everyone else. It's sheltered by tall pines and hugs a pristine green-blue lake—beautiful, yet all I see is that it's a good hundred yards from the nearest bathroom and separated from the main camp by a winding gravel road.

That night, we join the other campers in the lodge for the opening ceremony, and the director leads us in singing *Taps*.

"Day is done, gone the sun, from the lake, from the hills, from the sky; All is well, safely rest, God is nigh."

I tuck these words like a pebble in my pocket. If I could feel the brush of God in the house I shared with Dave, with its clutter of memories and broken hopes, then certainly I'll feel God here in this clean and open night air. I kiss the kids goodnight, and they drift easily into sleep. I'm about to doze off myself when I'm startled by the haunting call of a loon. I've never heard such a sound. It's a sort of wail that echoes across the lake and bounces against something inside me. After it fades, I reach for my phone and look up the meaning of the loon as a totem. According to *Animal Speak*, the haunting cry signifies that old hopes and dreams are about to come to the surface. Its message is: don't compromise again or you may find yourself haunted. The loon's cry calls forth all that we've ignored.

One might argue that *loon* also describes a silly or foolish person, but I don't feel foolish. I feel moved. And strengthened.

It doesn't last. By noon on the second day, Jed has worn down my nerves with demands, tantrums, and tears. We walk to the lake, and I manage to give him a quick hug before plunging into the water, where it makes sense that my face is wet. I wish I could say *I'm sorry, Jed*. I know how desperately he wants us all together. When he was a toddler, he loved to walk between Dave and me, wrapping one arm around our knees and pulling us close. He's the middle child and has always seemed happiest in the middle of his mom and dad.

Thankfully, April distracts him. She runs to the water's edge, points at the ground, and yells, "Look Jed, it's a perfectly good hole!" I sit beside them as they play, and I stare at the hole. What a metaphor it seems for my life. Is there a way to be in this dark place and know that it's perfectly good?

On the second night, the kids are once again asleep when I hear a different sound. Footsteps. They're slow and deliberate, coming closer and closer to the window. I have it slightly open, and through the screen the noise is unmistakable. I bolt upright and pull the curtain aside to peek out. I can't see anything, but I know what I heard. Every horror movie ever made begins playing; I see ax murderers and the flash of a white mask, I hear the thud of bloodthirsty zombies, the whir of a chainsaw. Like any true urbanite, I'm convinced that the most heinous crimes happen in the middle of nowhere. I peek again. Nothing. I remember that there's a motion-controlled light on the corner of the cabin. It's not on. But the noise is still there, sounding very close through the thin wood wall. Why isn't the light coming on? The footsteps sound human, but whatever it is can't be human if the light isn't on. I force myself to lie back down, heart racing. It's an animal, that's all. But I don't feel any better. I wait on high alert until there is nothing more to hear, then I grab my iPod, put my earbuds in, and listen to the Boston Pops Orchestra play *Les Miserables* until I fall asleep.

I stick close to the lodge the following day, made safe by sunshine, staff members, and internet access. That's when I overhear the director and head counselor talking about a bear. It's been years since they've spotted one, but there was a sighting the day before. I remember the bag of garbage sitting on my screened-in porch and realize what my late-night visitor was. I tell the director about the footsteps and, to my surprise, he offers us new lodging. The main house, located next to the lodge, with a bathroom and full kitchen, is available and it's ours for no extra charge.

"How nice of you," I say, flustered. "But that's not necessary. We'll be fine." I don't want to be a charity case. I thank him and turn away, then stop. What's the matter with me? This is a vacation, not a competition.

"Actually, I would really like that." I rush to tell the kids and after packing our things, we spend the rest of the afternoon spreading out on our individual beds, or sprawled on the full-length sofa, loudly announcing to each other that we are going to use the *indoor plumbing!*

Remembering my messages from the loon, I'm eager to look up the meaning of a bear visitation. I return to *Animal Speak* and learn that the bear, and particularly its ability to hibernate, reminds us to go within to find resources for survival and to make decisions of power. A bear totem can also be a reminder to not hide away or hibernate too long.

I wonder why it's so hard for me to see the simple act of moving to a new cabin as a decision of power, rather than weakness. What is the part of me that wants to hide away and not ask for help, or admit that I'm needy? I'm suddenly flooded with memories of the fear and homesickness I felt when I was fifteen years old and went to northern Michigan for band camp. The setting is so similar, and so is the way I compare myself to others, assuming that everyone else has "it" all figured out.

"Aren't you scared?" I wanted to ask those teenage girls who sat beside me in the flute section. I still want to ask that of practically everyone I meet.

When Logan plops next to me on the knotty pine sofa, I decide to admit this. I reach for him and say, "I'm scared because I don't have a husband."

"Mom, you're a strong, independent woman."

I look at him closely to see if he's joking, but his face is earnest. "I'm not invincible, you know."

"Neither is a husband," he says, and squeezes my hand.

When it's time for us to go home, my car experiences a mysterious electrical glitch, and the entire console goes dead. I can drive, but I have no gas gauge, no speedometer, no radio, no indicator lights. We travel in an eerie blank silence, more pronounced for me because the kids are happy to be reunited with their iPods and headphones, leaving me in the quiet. Into this stillness, I invite God.

What shows up is a recent memory involving our neighbor, who is rather eccentric. She lives alone, and has an elaborate web of chains and padlocks rigged from her porch posts to her front door. Recently, as I was getting into my car with April, she approached us.

"Someone broke into my house," she blurted. April leaned forward, listening intently, and I cringed. I didn't want her to have nightmares. "I know this because I found a loaf of bread on my counter and I don't eat bread. Someone was inside poking around!"

When she finally went back inside, I looked worriedly at April. Her face was wrinkled in confusion. I searched for words to comfort her but she exclaimed, "Did you hear that? She doesn't eat bread!"

Did you hear that? While I was focused on the burglar, April was fascinated by the bread. Could it be so simple? Could a sense of wonder and curiosity and deep listening be the key to bringing God into focus? If God is present in all things (and how can it be otherwise?) then maybe it's my lens that needs to shift.

So when school begins, I try to bring a new focus to our schedule. We're adjusting, but it feels far from routine. I'm too easily overwhelmed by dinner, homework, bath time, and bedtime, and often feel outnumbered and outsmarted by the kids.

One night, Jed refuses to do his schoolwork, and helplessness squeezes my chest. When Jed was four, Dave and I attended a support group for parents of kids with oppositional defiance disorder. We learned that natural consequences are the key to discipline. I can't think clearly. What are the natural consequences if Jed won't fill out this worksheet?

"I guess you don't care about your homework," I say, "so let's just throw it away." And I rip the paper into shreds.

Jed stares at me, then throws himself on the floor, thrashing and screaming. My uncertainty only grows. I can't put him in a time-out, so I put myself in one by escaping to my bedroom. I hide behind the closed door; I know that I took a wrong turn, and I have no idea how to get back on track.

Moments later Logan slides a note under the door that says, *Mom, I think that was very mean. I understand that you are frustrated with him, but I still think that was a little xtreme.*

I'm a failure—correction, a *mean* failure. I need a nine-year-old's help. How will I ever do this alone?

I slide off the bed onto my knees and lay my forehead against the white chenille bedspread. Dave no longer lives here, so he won't be barging into the room. I no longer need a lock on the door. I no longer want one. I want to live openly, beyond secrets and shame. I want to stop pretending that I know what I'm doing, because I don't.

When Jed was born, my labor proceeded so fast and furious that he was nearly born in the hospital elevator. The intensity of it had me screaming, "I can't do it!"

"You *are* doing it," the midwife answered calmly. And so I was. Yet it wasn't just me. No one could feel the supernal force of that moment and doubt the presence of God. But what about now?

I lift my head. Of course there's no one there. Only God.

What if God leaves me too?

19 Purple Prose

As a journalism major at Indiana University, one of my classes was magazine feature writing. The instructor's first name was Barth; he had a prestigious list of national bylines and was flamboyant, arrogant, brilliant, and brutal. In this class there was no collegial sharing of clever ideas and well-turned phrases, only students cowering before the demigod from New York City who was willing to slum with us for a semester. For our final article, we had to write a feature on a local personality or celebrity. I don't remember what descriptions I used, but I'll never forget the slash of purple marker across the page and, in the margin, the words UGH! PURPLE PROSE. THIS MAKES ME SICK!

What I had proudly believed to be inspired and uniquely descriptive writing was, according to Barth, unnecessarily flowery and extravagant. It was a smackdown I needed, a reminder that the romantic in me had no place beside the journalist. One of us had to die. But how could it be the girl who had been filling notebooks with love poems and quotes since junior high? I still have a journal from 1982 with the carefully-copied words of Elizabeth Barrett Browning: *How do I love thee? Let me count the ways. I love thee to the depth and breadth and height my soul can reach, when feeling out of sight for the ends of being and ideal grace. . . .*

I thought I could be both hard-nosed and soft-hearted. Like anyone who has never allowed herself to feel, I believed that passion could be parsed. Perhaps that was my first and most fatal mistake. What if, instead of shrinking into compliance, I'd said "Screw you, Barth! I want to write novels, and I'll be as flowery and exaggerated as I want." Because isn't it better to over-effuse and express yourself than to never say how you feel?

I don't know. I took the quiet route. I finished my novel in stolen, guilty parcels of time, carefully inching my way along, afraid to admit how important it was to me, and ultimately anxious about how loud and messy my characters were. As they came to life, they became more willful, screaming and swearing at one another, spilling secrets and telling lies, while I watched from a safe distance. I could close the cover on them like you would shut a door against a naughty child. They were me, but not me. Once, when I was the guest author at a book group discussion, one of the readers commented that so many sad things happen to my fictional family. I was startled and thought, but isn't that life? Don't you see it? Don't you *feel* it? Meanwhile, I could feel and say anything on the page, but not in real situations. Not with Dave.

As a journalism student, I tried to kill off the romantic in me, but now, when she should be dead, I feel her stirring. She sits up and says, *No, Barth, the facts aren't enough.* And as the wife who suffered the betrayal, I raise my hand in agreement; I too refuse to believe that emotion doesn't add anything to my story. I'm all for adding blame, indignation, and outrage. Author Natalie Babbitt said, "Facts are the barren branches on which we hang the dear, obscuring foliage of our dreams." Hang away, I say! The bleak truth shows itself soon enough—like when my friend Megan, who has known Dave for twenty years, gives me this warning, "Don't mediate. Dave is a professional persuader and very good at his job. He's used to getting his way." And Abigail, nodding in agreement, adds, "He doesn't care about you." Does it get more barren than that? Sure, it hurts, but everyone needs someone who doesn't parse words, who gives it to you straight.

Against the backdrop of this stark truth—DAVE DOESN'T CARE ABOUT ME—comes the confirmation from Logan that Dave has a girlfriend. It's no surprise. What is a surprise is that she's not Allison. Her name is Beth. She's twelve years younger than Dave, with no kids, and she made dinner for them at Dave's apartment.

Next comes an email from my dad. This is another surprise, since I rarely hear from him. He writes that he's scheduled for a risky heart surgery. After years of living with a severely enlarged heart that was pumping at only fifteen percent capacity, he's getting a new aortic valve.

He admits that he's afraid. He wants to get right with God. He writes, *I am fully aware that I have been a terrible father and have failed you in many ways. I ask for your forgiveness.*

Here it is! The admission, the entreaty, the long-anticipated moment when he becomes the father I've always wanted and I bask in his love and pride. But I feel hollow. I don't know how to respond. Finally I reply the way I think a responsible, healthy adult would:

> *Dear Dad, You are saying the words I've waited years to hear, but they're not living up to my expectations. Mixed with my relief and gratitude at reading this is also a lot of pain. I'm angry that I didn't get to know you as a dad. I'm sad that you never knew me. I've struggled for years with feeling invisible and unworthy, with anxiety and fears of abandonment. But I do appreciate your email and will pray for your health.*

I hate my words. I sound stiff and formal, stingy and petulant. Still, I'm being honest and expressing what I've never dared to say. He writes:

Tammy, Thank you so very much for your email. The guilt I have felt over the past years has served as justification for me to withdraw and feel unwanted and unworthy. I do not know how to be a dad. I must rely on you to teach me if you are willing. I can still learn if I survive the surgery.

I do not want to rehash all the sins of my past. I feel that God has made me a new creature, and I want to go from this day forward to become a better person and dad.

Translation: he doesn't really want to know in what ways he hurt me. He wants to lay the word *forgiveness* down like a token in a game. He wants to use it to get out of jail free. He wants to start with a clean slate. *If* he lives. Angrily, I whip off a reply:

But I'm the kid! Why do I have to teach you what to do? This makes me feel weary and resentful.

Then I get scared. I've gone too far. I'm being unfair. He may die! We have one chance to get this right and I'm quibbling. I take out a book on forgiveness, hoping to read something that will open my heart in a burst of loving white light. I find this from Robert Holden: *In essence, true forgiveness is the willingness to believe 1. you are whole. 2. no one can threaten or take away your wholeness.*

That afternoon I get a terrible migraine. I still have to pick up the kids from school, and when Logan asks me what's wrong, I tell him I'm afraid because I told my dad I'm angry with him. He takes my hand. "You were being honest, Mom, and if he can't listen, then it's his problem. Besides," he adds, "there's nothing he can do to you."

Despite my fog of pain, I hear him and have a flash of gratitude for his wisdom and uncanny claircognizance. I am whole, and no one can threaten my wholeness. From that place, I ask my heart what it wants to say. There is no dear, obscuring foliage in its immediate answer, which I send to my dad: *Just listen to me.*

So we begin a tentative, benign correspondence. My brother Bryan has told him about Dave and the divorce, so I write little about it; instead, I write about my kids, whom he's never met. He shares that he likes dogs, cherry trees, flea markets, and fishing. In his way, he tries to comfort me.

Dear Tammy, I have been thinking about you and just wanted to wish you a good day. I know you are facing a lot, but there is always good with the bad. I used to think life was hills and valleys with both high and low points. I have since learned that it is more like a railroad track. One rail may be difficult and hard but the other rail that runs beside it is full of good and blessings. I hope your day is full of good things and many blessings. Love, Dad.

Tammy, I don't sleep very well so a lot of mornings I go down to the marina about 4:00 a.m. I really enjoy the mornings, watching nature waking up and the beautiful sunrise. A couple weeks ago an eagle flew by about fifty feet above the water. I sit there with my coffee and give God thanks for another day.

Wednesday night Marilyn and I are cooking the dinner at church. We are having a ham and bean dish that I found in a Taste of Home that is really good. It has lots of ham and about seven different kinds of beans along with ketchup, brown sugar, onion, Worcestershire sauce. Marilyn is making home-made brown bread, which everyone raves about.

Hello again. Attached are some pictures of the trees in our front yard. A few weeks ago they were dead looking and desolate. Today they are alive and beautiful, none of which could be possible had they not gone through the difficult time of winter. Perhaps there is a lesson for all of us in this.

At one point I write:

Dad, I have always had the weird feeling that some other person was living my life because I don't have many memories at all of being little, and most of the ones I do have are of being anxious. I wondered if you have memories of me as a kid and what they are.

Tammy, you asked about your childhood. The thing I remember most was the snowmobiling when we used to pull you kids around in a sled behind the snowmobile. We went on quite a few camping trips which were always a lot of fun. Specific things I really don't remember. I was a lousy dad and sort of rambled along without really developing a close relationship. I regret that very much now. Also, I can hardly remember what I did this morning and a lot of the past is totally a blank spot. Maybe this is my subconscious way of escaping. I do remember you playing the flute and you were always an excellent student. You never caused any kind of trouble.

I gather up these pieces and savor them; they're lifesaver candies against a growling empty stomach. When my dad writes that he started reading my novel and that he's going to order more copies to give to his friends at church, I experience a moment of fullness. Then it's gone. I'm still hungry. *What is wrong with me?*

❀

My dad comes through his surgery with flying colors. After that, our correspondence tapers off. I wait for him to mention my novel again, but he never does.

I tell Walter this at our next session.

"What were you hoping for?" I hear in his tone the slightest tinge of surprise and disbelief.

I don't want to answer. Isn't it obvious?

Walter waits.

"The book pretty much lays out how a teenage girl feels about being abandoned by her father. I thought it would make him understand me."

"And then what?" he prompts.

"At least he admits he was a lousy dad. He says he regrets it. But I guess I want him to say he's sorry."

"Dave said he's sorry. Did it mean anything? Is that really all you want?"

I consider this. "There's something about Dave's apology and my dad's that doesn't change anything. I thought I'd feel better and I don't. But I'd like to be able to show my kids that they can forgive their dad."

"Show them by doing it, by living it." Walter suggests that I write a list of what he calls my negative beliefs. Bitterly, I shove the dreamer in me aside and take out a blank piece of paper. These are the facts that seem to be irrefutable:

Everyone will let me down.

People leave me because they don't see who I am.

People leave me because they DO see who I am.

I'm not special enough.

No one understands me.

Dave never cared about me.

My dad never cared about me.

I'll end up alone because (here's the big one) love is never enough.

Ugh. Purple prose. I make myself sick.

20 A Slow Unraveling

The first time Paul came to my apartment, he used a cane, and the first time I went to his apartment, he was able to cross from his kitchen to his living room by holding onto the walls. Now, despite intense physical therapy and the use of an expensive electrical stimulation device on his leg muscles, he has to rely wholly on his wheelchair. As a result, he's more comfortable downtown, where the sidewalks have reliable curb-cuts, and the buildings are accessible. At his place there's an elevator, and grab-bars in the shower, and the bed is positioned so he can easily transfer to it from his chair. But I get claustrophobic in the high-rise. I'm an Earth-bound Taurus and a homebody, and I love to putter around my own house. So we figure out how to get him up the seven front steps into my first floor. With the railing on his good side and me on the other, we manage the transfer, but the effort exhausts us both. Mostly I don't mind. Paul keeps me company while I work to make the house mine. I paint April's room and hang new curtains. I weed the yard and carefully choose perennials for the shady spots along the fence. I do the things Dave didn't want to do, and Paul is there to listen and advise, to smile at me and listen to me talk. We order takeout and watch movies, and he rubs my legs and feet and kisses me in a way that makes me feel both precious and lethal. He's there the afternoon I come in from the backyard to find a squirrel sitting on the kitchen table. Even though he gets annoyed by my hysterics when the squirrel bolts into the living room and sits on the sofa, he helps me get it out, and eventually we share a laugh. Never mind that Paul probably isn't any more interested in my house projects than Dave was. He's interested in *me*, and his willingness to spend time with me makes me feel supported.

"He sounds like your pet," Abigail says, and I'm mortified because it's true. I'm guilty of wanting a witness to my life, and he seems happy to be my audience. Because he can't come or go without my help, he is literally a captive audience, and that makes me *captivating*.

Is it so wrong to want to be center stage? I've always been the quiet one, the observer, the new girl waiting to be welcomed. And yet wasn't Dave willing to let me shine? On my fortieth birthday, Dave threw a surprise party for me. He told me we were going to see a play at a local theater. Once there, we were rushed to the front row and just as I was noticing that I knew *everyone* in the audience, Dave stepped onto the stage and announced that the performance would be a one-act play I had written. Not only had he staged the play, but he had compiled a collection of my short stories into a book and everyone would get a copy. I was stunned, flattered, honored, and instantly filled with dread. Where had he gotten my drafts? Were they the correct ones? Were they ready to be shared? I was so worried I could hardly concentrate on the play, though it seemed to go well. Afterward, friends raved about what an amazing thing Dave had done. Several husbands joked that he'd forever doomed the rest of them to fall short in the birthday present department. I struggled to take it all in. Finally I stole a moment alone in the women's bathroom and took a good long look at myself. Why couldn't I relax into this once-in-a-lifetime event? Dave was the most thoughtful husband imaginable. Everyone said so.

Paul and I are on Chicago's lakefront path, near Burnham Harbor, on our way to have dinner at an outdoor cafe that overlooks the marina. It's a beautiful evening, and the boats bob like colorful toys on the blue-green water. The tall masts of the yachts remind me of something I heard in *What the Bleep Do We Know?* It's a 2004 film that looks at the spiritual connection between quantum physics and consciousness and suggests that the universe is constructed from thought rather than matter.

I turn to Paul. "You know, there's a theory that when explorers first came in their ships, the Native Americans didn't even see them approaching because they didn't know what ships were. They had no mental reference for them, so they were literally invisible to them. Isn't that *fascinating*?" I start talking with my hands, the way I do when I'm excited. "Apparently our brains are bombarded with so much more information than we can process that we have to choose what to allow in. We filter out information that's unfamiliar." I pause to take a breath, but I'm just getting started.

Paul points to a nearby high-rise. "I think that building is new," he says impassively.

I feel the wind leave my sails as if I'm one of those ships, as if I'm invisible to Paul. I wait, but he doesn't say anything more, and I know he won't. He looks at the solid structures before him, while my eyes are on the wide expanse of the lake. When we look at one another, time seems to stand still, locking us in our own new world. But increasingly, when we manage to break our gaze, we're looking in different directions.

Surely this is okay. Isn't it? The poet Rumi writes that even between the closest people infinite distances must exist. It must be the mark of a healthy relationship to allow differences. But in this moment I don't feel close. We arrive at the restaurant, order our dinner, and eat in silence. I don't have anything to talk about. Maybe I'm sulking, or maybe—and this thought starts lapping at me like the waves against the dock—maybe if I don't carry the conversation, there won't be one.

After a while Paul grins and says, "I'm going to call you Helen." When I look confused he reaches over and taps my forehead. "It must be hell in there."

I manage a weak smile but this ship that is me is now taking on water. It's the old familiar flood. Tammy is too sensitive. Tammy overanalyzes. Tammy is too much work.

Maybe I don't know what I want. My theory of love is that two people should equal more than the sum of their parts. Certainly Dave and I seemed bigger together in the world. Paul and I seem greater alone, more diminished in public. In either case, I'm not sure what I add. What am I not factoring in? What integral piece is missing? All I know is that I can't break my attachment to Paul. He's a security blanket, a puppy dog, and a crack addiction all rolled into one. He's my flashlight through the darkness, but the battery is running low.

One night, I'm out with two girlfriends at a neighborhood bar. We're talking about our relationships with the men in our lives and I admit that Paul hasn't read my novel. There is a pause. My friend Suzie reaches into her purse and takes out her calendar. She rips a blank page from the back of it and writes in block letters: HE DIDN'T EVEN READ YOUR BOOK.

"Take this home and hang it on your bathroom mirror."

I'm abashed but can't stop myself from defending him. "Don't you think a true soul mate is the one who forces you to look at yourself?" I launch into a lengthy, convoluted explanation about how Paul's lack of interest in my writing only serves to make me stronger because I have to rely on myself for validation. I sound ridiculous and I know it.

The next time Paul is at my house, I'm moody and quiet. Eventually he moves to sleep on the sofa and I don't stop him. I can't decide if he's being sensitive or punitive. I toss and turn, and in the morning I kneel beside him. He looks as if he hasn't slept either.

"I used to feel adored by you," he says. "Now I feel like you can take or leave me."

We both begin to cry. I don't want to hurt Paul. I don't want to be the one to deliver the blow. I wish I could articulate something Abigail said to me about a slow unraveling between people, that if you can part gently then you won't bring ragged edges to your next relationship. This is what I want. But is it possible?

"What are we going to do?" I ask.

Paul shrugs. "Ride this horse until it bucks us off."

That sounds more frightening than a slow unraveling. I take his hand and we cling to each other. I pray that we can let go slowly and gently. I won't survive another severing.

21 An Ever-Fixed Mark

S itting in a sterile waiting room at the Daley Center in Chicago with my journal in my lap, waiting to be called into mediation, I'm unexpectedly calm. I close my eyes and envision the word *media-tion*. Insert a T into it—T for Tammy—and it becomes meditation. I'm putting myself in the center, bringing my attention back to where it belongs. There's nothing I can do but sit in the middle of this and allow it to unfold.

It's been brought to my attention (thank you, Walter) that I operate under what could be called hypervigilance. It's a belief that if I don't pay attention carefully enough or do or say the right thing at the right time, the world will fall apart and it will be all my fault. Conversely, if I do everything correctly, I will be loved. This sounds ridiculous, but . . . *yes*. I do feel this way. It's very tiring, and it hasn't stopped me from becoming a cog in the machine that is the Cook County Divorce Court System. Lawyers and mediators and psychologists and vocational experts and ultimately a judge will decide how often I can see my children, which holidays I'll spend alone, and what the payout should be for my years of wifely service.

There's one thing I'm certain about: no matter what Dave does or doesn't do, I'm not negotiating or compromising on the mother I choose to be. The rest I turn over to a power much greater than I. As

I do, I feel, paradoxically, a surge of power, and for a nanosecond I glimpse what will become a growing certainty for me: surrender does not mean being a doormat.

The mediator is a middle-aged woman, and we meet in her small, cozy office at a round table that is pushed into one corner. The walls are covered with children's drawings, and though I'm not clear why her job would bring her into such close contact with kids (we were told to leave ours home), the gallery of rainbows, puffy clouds, and cartwheeling stick figures creates an air of lightheartedness I wasn't expecting. She lets me begin and I tell her that we are unable to finalize a parenting schedule. Dave insists on fifty-fifty residential custody, but I won't agree. He's renting a friend's condo less than ten minutes away and, though it's comfortable and spacious enough for the kids, it's a temporary situation. It's not the kids' *home*. Besides, we both grew up with stay-at-home mothers and agreed it's important for me to be with the kids when they are not at school. This was a value we shared for more than a decade. Why does he get to decide something else?

"April is three years old," I say. "What will you do with her while you're at work?"

"Let me worry about that. Besides, you're going to have to work too."

I start to protest that writing books *is* work, but I stop myself. Dave will call it a hobby, not a career. Funny, I always felt that he was my biggest supporter. Now that's changed, and any sense of legitimacy I had withers away.

Dave continues to tell the mediator his babysitter plan. He'll find students from nearby Northeastern University who can drive the kids to school. He lays this out airily, oblivious to the fact that the dime-a-dozen caregivers he describes can't be found for under fifteen dollars an hour—an illogical price for us. I can't listen. I let my mind return to the movie I watched the previous night. In *Sense and Sensibility,* Marianne is heartbroken when Willoughby, the man she loves, callously reveals a history of debauchery. But Marianne's devastation goes beyond the actions of one man. It's the shattering of her belief in ideal love that nearly kills her. The words of William Shakespeare had been her North Star:

> *Love is not love*
> *Which alters when it alteration finds*
> *Or bends with the remover to remove.*
> *O no! It is an ever-fixed mark*
> *That looks on tempests and is never shaken.*

Dave intends to remove the very core of who I am. Without my children, my ever-fixed marks, who and what am I?

I focus on a drawing of a fat yellow sun on the office wall. I trust that the sun is an ever-fixed mark. I trust that I am my children's mother and that nothing or no one can change that. I have my writing. My God has me. These are immovable marks. Like Marianne, I have to put aside other ideals in order to glimpse that what Shakespeare is describing can only be Divine love. Around this small round table on the nineteenth floor of the Daley Center, we are merely mortals, and we are stalled.

We set the parenting schedule aside and move to a standard clause in the parenting agreement that prohibits overnight guests of the opposite sex when the kids are present. Dave wants the clause left out, and I imagine his girlfriend Beth cooking not only the kids' dinners, but their breakfasts. Then I imagine a string of Beths. I shake my head adamantly. The mediator suggests that what Dave is asking may not be in the best interest of the kids, and he goes into the hall, calls his lawyer, and demands that she be replaced.

Oh Willoughby, Willoughby! When Dave returns, I shut my notebook, tuck it and my pen into my purse, and stand.

"Thank you," I say to the mediator. "I'm finished." And I leave. As I await the elevator, I wish that saying those words aloud, *I'm finished,* could make it so. But how can I be finished? I'm going to be told what kind of job to get. Worse, I just walked out of mediation, which means we're headed for trial, and I'm terrified. But I'm finished being told how to feel, finished assuming that Dave knows best, that he is automatically the one to be applauded.

I don't speak to Dave for several days, until the afternoon I get an email from my attorney. It's another court order, this one requiring me to undergo psychiatric testing. I haven't even met with the vocational expert I've been ordered to see, and now Dave has paid five thousand dollars more to have me psychiatrically evaluated. I'm heartsick, but not completely blindsided. Paul warned me that this is a common divorce attorney tactic to draw the process out, and that Dave's attorney can be counted on to pull every dirty trick. Still, five thousand dollars? To accomplish what exactly?

"There is no goal aside from intimidating you," Paul says.

When Dave comes to pick up the kids for his evening with them, I hiss at him through clenched teeth. "Psychiatric testing? What the hell, Dave? You think I'm an unfit mother?"

He looks genuinely surprised. "Of course not. You're a great mother." He calls for the kids to hurry up. "Got your toothbrush?" he asks Logan as they hustle past me out the door. He smiles and waves at me and they're gone.

I'm shaken. Never mind Dave's friendliness. He so clearly despises me and I don't know why. How far will he go? How can I protect myself against him? He's incredibly creative and competitive. He can charm or bully his way through anything, and I'm certain he'll be able to do the same thing in court.

I don't stand a chance.

22 Final Farewell

I was always an excellent student. That's what my dad wrote in his email to me. Certainly I got good grades all through high school, but I'm not sure I *excelled* in school. I was not Dave, who had straight A's all through college and whose name is etched on a bronze tablet on the wall of the Main Library at the University of Illinois. When it came to my college exams, I lacked the stamina to pull all-nighters or attend study groups or decipher the broken English of my statistics class assistant instructor. There was one time I tried to stay up all night studying; I took a NoDoz pill that made me feel like I was having a heart attack. I spent the wee hours nauseated and shaky, which resulted in being less, not more, prepared. Another time I walked into my 8:00 a.m. Behavioral Psychology class to find the teacher passing out the midterm exam. It would count as one-third of my grade, and I didn't know it was being given that day. I guessed at all the answers and scraped by with a D.

When the time comes for me to be tested by a vocational expert and a psychiatrist, I'm not sure if I need to prepare, or what that would even entail. The best thing I can do is to stay calm, so I schedule a Healing Touch appointment with Janet.

"How did you learn to do this?" I ask her after our session. I still don't understand how the simple, gentle movement of her hands over my body can make me feel lighter and at the same time more grounded. I expect her to say that she was born with psychic abilities, but she says she is no more psychic than anyone. She pulls a brochure from her bag. It's for a beginning-level Healing Touch training the following month.

At home, I read about the program with a strange sense of knowing, as if a decision has already been made to embark on this path. Energy healing has to be one of the strangest, most far-out things I've ever encountered, but it makes sense to me on a deep level. If I become certified in Healing Touch, I too could work at a doctor's office or wellness center. I could earn an income, and still continue to write. So I send in my registration form and enjoy a small surge of confidence.

My vocational assessment takes place in the suburbs, in a sterile vanilla office with nothing but a round conference table and two chairs. The expert introduces himself as Ron. Just Ron, with no distracting title or credentials. He's a tall but slouchy middle-aged man, with thinning dark hair and wire-rimmed glasses. We get right to business. He asks about my sleeping habits and whether I have trouble getting up in the morning. The fact that I'm in the process of a divorce and not taking antidepressants seems noteworthy; he jots something on his pad.

I don't mention the sleeping pills, which I've mostly stopped taking. Instead, I tell him about my college degree and that I recently finished a novel.

"I was in the process of looking for an agent when the divorce began," I explain. "And before that I worked as a copywriter." I hand him my resume. I've been a good girl and included just the facts, even though, when it comes to past jobs, I think in terms of stories, not skills. Would Ron be interested in my stories?

Like when I was sixteen years old, working third shift as a waitress at a Bob Evans restaurant, standing for hours at the counter in the middle of the night, my feet aching, my fingers mindlessly rolling silverware into paper napkins. An old man sat on the last stool, with a cup of coffee in front of him. His eyes were closed and he seemed to be dozing, but then a low chuckle shook him. He cracked open one eye and looked at me. "God told me a joke," he said. I believed him, not caring if he was crazy.

Or when I was an intern at a TV station in Toledo, Ohio, and was sent to cover the local school council meeting—groundbreaking news! It was my first time on camera, and I discovered that the footage of the reporter is taken *after* the interview. So when the cameraman finished filming the president of the council talking about two new bus routes being added, he then shot me, alone, listening intently to an empty chair. I learned to feign interest.

Or when I was a copywriter at a marketing agency in Chicago. I worked on the McDonald's account and often went to McDonald's corporate headquarters in Oak Brook, Illinois to taste new products. Even though I was a vegetarian, I was told that I had better take a bite of the new McBLT burger "if I know what's good for me," which was, I thought, an interesting choice of words. I ate the burger.

See Ron? Aren't anecdotes more illuminating than dates and duties? But I don't say any of this. I simply answer his questions, and though both the questions and the answers are duller than dull, Ron does a lot of thoughtful nodding, and several times says *interesting, interesting.* Then I describe my idea to become an energy medicine practitioner. I talk about the Healing Touch training that will be held at Swedish Covenant Hospital and he says, "Hmm, I don't know much about that field," which tempts me to ask how he came to be known as a job expert. I wonder if it was anything like becoming an ordained minister through the internet. $29.99 for expertise in ten areas. $59.99 lets you claim to know everything!

Ron shuffles a few papers, takes off his glasses, and smiles at me. "You certainly have a lot of energy," he says. I don't know if he is being literal, or attempting a joke about my new career plan. I wait for him to give me a list of jobs he thinks I should pursue—what color *is* my parachute?—but he doesn't. We finish earlier than the allotted time. "I'll be writing up a report," he says, ushering me toward the door.

"I'll be writing a blog," I say. I'm able to joke now that I'm leaving. I'm angry though—angry that I was put through this ridiculous waste-of-time charade; angry that Dave continues to take a flame-thrower to our future by recklessly racking up legal fees; angry that after each hurdle I clear, another appears.

My next test is with the psychiatrist. This time I'm downtown in the small, eerily quiet office of Dr. Sarah Jones, using a number-two pencil to fill in more than five hundred little circles on the Minnesota Multiphasic Personality Inventory. The true/false statements range from easy (*Evil spirits possess me at times*) to uncertain (*My father is a good man; At times I feel like swearing*) to baffling (*I used to like drop-the-handkerchief*). They're written with varying wording but reveal recurring themes: one around whether I like to start fires, others related to nightmares, small animals, and talking to strangers.

It would be easy to feel unhinged at this point, but Dr. Jones is an easygoing woman who looks like she should work in a bakery, or maybe at a Joann Fabrics store. We talk a bit, and while I suppose I'm being evaluated during our chitchat, I'm able to relax a little. I compliment her necklace, a large smoky quartz stone pendant, and she says, "I wear it in court for good energy. Another trick I use, especially with attorneys like your husband's, is to stare at their third eye. It really freaks them out."

I gape at her. I didn't see that coming.

"I learned a trick for talking to narcissists," I blurt. "Cross your arms in front of your solar plexus, because that's where a narcissist will hook into you energetically. To sort of feed off you. The energy healer I go to taught me that." I stop, afraid that I've said too much and that this comment will affect my test results.

But Dr. Jones nods earnestly. "I'll have to remember that one," she says.

The tests I've taken seem as insubstantial as the paper they're printed on, assuming they were ever printed. I never see them. Instead, Dave's attorney sends over a new proposal: Dave is offering to work from home every Wednesday during the summer in order to be home with the kids. While I'm looking over the paperwork, Logan comes home and says he needs five dollars for a field trip the next day.

"I was supposed to turn it in already and if I don't bring it tomorrow, I can't go," he says.

I sigh, exasperated. "Why didn't you ask your dad when you were there last night?" It's a small thing, but I'm annoyed that Dave leaves these matters to me.

Logan glares at me, his hands on his hips, and says, "Mom, this is no time for your stubbornness!"

While I scrounge through my purse to come up with five dollars in coins, I think that maybe he's right. I am stubborn. I'm also angry that Dave has managed to make even this last detail a game of chicken, so that if I don't flinch, all the fallout will be entirely my fault. I'll be the one blamed for drawing it out, just as I'm to blame for my systemic lack of passion and the contempt and resentment I apparently subjected him to.

I take another look at the papers. I really hate the idea of being without my kids half the time. Honestly, it scares me. If I'm not being a mother, what am I? What if I can't remember or recover myself, or even if I do, what if switching between roles proves too hard? Instead of excelling at either, I'll be a mediocre mom and a half-assed writer. I'll have to find out sooner or later. So I open my laptop and send an email to Scott, telling him that Dave wins—he can have one more overnight each week with the kids.

All that remains is one last appearance before the judge. My pastor offers to come downtown with me for it. She's been through her own divorce, and she says that for her, declaring out loud that the marriage was finished was emotional. But I decline. I'm not sure what I'll feel, but it can't be worse than what's come already. I can face it on my own.

This act of independence becomes almost a badge of honor. I even fight the urge to call Paul, though I can't help recalling all the times he met me at the courthouse and waited for me at the cafe across the street, sometimes even ordering my coffee so it would be ready when I walked in. Today I cross the wide courtyard alone, past the bubbling water fountain and looming Picasso statue that looks to me like a giant fossilized poodle, and shuffle through the metal detectors behind a string of men I assume are lawyers. The man in front of me takes off his belt before he goes through security, revealing the rumpled back of his white shirt and his empty belt loops. That, plus the visible outline of his T-shirt, feels overly intimate and makes me look away. Once I pass through the metal detector without setting off any alarms, I wait at the elevator bank for the car that will shoot me up to the thirty-second floor to Judge Garcia's courtroom. He's a gentle looking, soft-spoken man—not at all what I would imagine to be "judge-looking." I like him, but he's been the arbiter of my shattered marriage and, no offense to him, I never want to see him again.

As usual, Dave and I give one another a terse hello and wait, quiet and separate. As I've done so often in this same courtroom, I fix my eyes on the phrase mounted in small silver letters on the wall: *In God We Trust*. When the final moment arrives, it's more pomp than circumstance. We're called up to the bench, the judge asks us to affirm aloud that we agree to the dissolution of our marriage, the clerk puts a stamp on a piece of paper, our history is filed away under a number, and my partner of twenty years is free of me.

I leave the federal building wondering if I should somehow

commemorate this moment. I have another urge to call Paul, but don't feel I *need* to, and I want to enjoy this subtle shift. I cross Randolph street, push through the revolving doors of the Corner Bakery, and treat myself to a large cinnamon latte.

The next morning a thunderstorm unleashes itself with a fury against the west-facing windows of my living room as I return from dropping the kids at school. I make a cup of tea and turn on Oprah Winfrey. After twenty-five years, she's ending her daytime talk show, and though I was never a regular viewer, she's a Chicago icon and media phenomenon, and I want to see today's show, which is titled *The Final Farewell*. I clearly remember watching Johnny Carson's last broadcast in 1992. Dave and I had recently moved in together, and we watched it on a giant Magnavox television that sat on shelves made of plywood and cinder blocks. The Johnny Carson show had been on my entire life, and when Johnny pulled up a stool and bid us "a very heartfelt goodnight," I felt as though I were losing a favorite uncle; I was unexpectedly bereft.

Today Oprah's message is equally personal. From an empty stage at Harpo Studios, just miles from my house, she stands in a pink dress and speaks only to me: "I know that I've never been alone, and you haven't either. That presence, that flow, some people call it grace, is working in my life at every single turn. And yours too, if you let it in. It's closer than your breath, and it is yours for the asking . . . Be still and know it."

For some reason I'm drawn to the floor, this floor that held me the night Dave delivered the blow, where I listened to Deva Premal songs over and over. There's a tangible sense of freedom and sur- render that comes from laying your body down. So I unroll my yoga mat, sink onto my back, and become still as I listen to Oprah. Like her theme song says, she's every woman and she's every voice in my head. The understanding Oprah says that everyone only wants to be seen and heard and know that they matter. The no-nonsense Oprah says, "Nobody but you is responsible for your life." The poor, abused black girl from Mississippi who became the richest woman in the world and calls her life a miracle looks me in the eye and says, "Your life is speaking to you. What is it saying?"

I roll over and lie with my cheek against the floor. I'm not ready for this question. It makes me tired. *What is my life saying?* I wish I knew, Oprah. I wish I knew.

23 The Price of Freedom

Free at last! Now that my divorce is over, I can finally be happy and put the whole contentious mess behind me. I'm in a new chapter of my life, and all is well. I recall the girls' weekend at the Lakeside Inn, when Ellen asked if Dave was leaving me, or if I was divorcing him. Well, it's official. I divorced him. Never again will I consider myself left. Instead, I've been *liberated*.

So where is the glorious sense of independence I expected? When do I get to dab on *savoir-faire* like an expensive perfume that every modern divorcee earns the right to wear? I suppose even new lives have to be incubated, hatched open and struggled against before moving forward with small wobbly steps.

My first Healing Touch training weekend reminds me how good it can feel to see with brand new eyes. About twenty students, mostly women and many nurses, gather at a cancer treatment center in a northern suburb to learn about the history and science behind energy therapy. The program is a fascinating mix of ancient wisdom and cutting edge quantum physics. Topics like intuition, higher sensory perception, and divine guidance are discussed matter-of-factly, the way a math teacher might break down a formula or a science teacher might review the periodic table. When one woman admits that she's had visions for years and was always afraid she wasn't normal, the instructor says, "Normal is a setting on a washing machine."

We begin our training by feeling the energy between our hands; we're instructed to grow it into a ball of qi that can be compressed or stretched or otherwise manipulated. I'm relieved that I'm able to sense a gentle, warm pulsation in my palms. Next we're encouraged to use our hands to feel the edges of one another's biofields. We practice by walking toward a partner, palms outstretched, until we detect a slight tingle or warmth or resistance. Everyone feels it in various ways, and the few students who are not kinesthetic and feel nothing are told to visualize the aura instead.

"The beauty of Healing Touch is that it is activated by your intention," says the instructor, a diminutive woman with long flowing gray hair and a Mona Lisa smile. "It's nice if you can detect differences in the aura, but it makes no difference if you can feel it or not. By tuning into your heart and setting an intention for healing, the energy will go where it's needed."

"What if the recipient doesn't believe in it?" one student asks.

"It's just as effective. It's proven to work on skeptics as well as believers."

We move on to experimenting with pendulums, watching for a clockwise spin when the pendulum is held over a chakra.

"What if it doesn't move?" I ask, nodding at the way my pendulum hangs frozen and stick straight from my hand. "How do I know if the chakra is flowing or congested?"

"Just ask," the instructor says enigmatically.

I glance around. I thought I *was* asking. Then I realize she means to ask Spirit, or God, or the energy itself. "Uh, okay." I pose the question in my mind and the pendulum moves.

I glance around again, this time wondering if anyone else is doubting the legitimacy of this, but everyone is peering at their own pendulums. Over the course of the day, whenever someone asks a question, the instructor repeats those two words—just ask—and it ignites the wick of something snarky and rebellious in me. I want to buddy up to one of the other students and grouse, "Nice gig huh, when you don't have to answer any questions!" But the Mona Lisa smile and confident knowingness that accompanies the instructor's words make me pause. I remind myself that I'm here to learn.

We spend the day studying the chakra system and discussing how to determine which healing techniques are called for, how to take a client's health history, and how to document a session. We also get plenty of time on the treatment table receiving Healing Touch, and I'm astounded by the significant energy shifts I experience at the hands of fellow students who are just as new to this as I am.

During one practice session, as another student sweeps her hands slowly down my body, inches from me but not touching, I drift into a relaxed state and have a powerful vision of two angels walking beside me. They're twelve feet tall, one man and one woman. The man has beautiful strong hands, like Paul, and he takes my hand and leads me to the edge of a cliff overlooking a beautiful valley and cozy village. I have the ability to look into every house and heart and feel the joy emanating from the people there as they dance and laugh and love. The woman turns to me. "All of this is yours," she says. "Stop playing small."

She should have told me to stop playing God. I take her words as a personal and sacred missive; truly, I appreciate the inspiration. But I can't resist swelling into grandiosity. What if it's also in my power to heal Paul, so he could somehow be mine as well? In my fantasies, if Paul regains his strength and mobility, he'll develop his own interests and hobbies, and we can somehow have a dynamic, supportive relationship.

When I return from my training, I ask Paul if he'd like to experience Healing Touch, merely as a way to help me reach my required one hundred practice hours. He agrees, and we fall into a weekly routine, getting together every Wednesday for a healing session, followed by dinner and a movie or early bedtime. At first he seems enthusiastic about the energy work, but before long I sense he's humoring me. He seems more bemused than genuinely curious. With a twinge of familiar annoyance, I wonder again what subject, if any, might rouse his curiosity. I won't admit to myself that I keep seeing him for all the wrong reasons, the greatest of these the hope that I'm some sort of miracle worker. The truth is so much more banal: I'm lonely. And I'm afraid to be officially alone.

Thankfully I have plenty to keep me busy. I'm on the fast track to reach my certification, determined to fly through all five levels of training in record time. A stack of metaphysical books appears next to my bed. There are reports to write and alternative modalities to experience as I make my way through the program.

The most significant commitment I make is to meditation. Twenty minutes, every morning. I dive into this with the zeal of a convert, convinced that, after all I've been through, I'll easily leapfrog past the foggy self-awareness of the masses into the realm of mystic. One rainy morning I take my usual seat on the sofa, pleased with the gentle rivulets of rainwater on the window pane, eager to sink into the pillows I've perfectly arranged behind my back. As I close my eyes and begin to focus on my breath, I feel my heart quicken. Like a crack of thunder, a flash of panic comes from nowhere and rocks me. It doesn't seem to be attached to a fearful thought; instead, it feels independent of me but at the same time encoded in every cell. I force myself to breathe. What am I afraid of? Nothing. Everything. This is terror, blind and pure, that bypasses the brain. I keep breathing, knowing instinctively that I can't outsmart it.

In time, it subsides. But it keeps happening. My stilled mind becomes a stage, and every fear I've ever had insists on prancing across it. I maintain my practice, but barely. When I'm not meditating, I pore over books and videos looking for answers. This can't be right. Where is the peace and serenity that meditation is supposed to unlock?

I find myself drawn back to a familiar conclusion: I must be doing it wrong.

Logan wants mac and cheese. Jed wants chicken nuggets. I agree to make both, even though boiling water for the pasta requires using the stove, and lately I've earned the title of microwave mama. Their meals are barely a step up from toast, but at least it's a step in the right direction.

"I'm uncomfortable," Logan says once we're all sitting at the dinner table.

"What's wrong?"

"Not now," he says. "I mean at Dad's. I don't like it. I can't fall asleep in my bed."

"Did this just start?" I ask, because they've been going to Dave's apartment for several months now.

He shrugs. "I feel better if I sleep on the sofa and Dad sits next to me."

"It's not easy being in two different houses, is it? It'll get better. I promise." I can only hope this is true. I wouldn't enjoy schlepping my things back and forth, but then kids are supposed to be more resilient than adults. I make a mental note to send some things along in his backpack the next time he goes to Dave's, maybe his favorite PJs or a new CD for his CD player.

When I drop the kids off a few days later, Logan asks if I'll go in and see the apartment.

I hesitate.

"No offense, Mom, but Dad is better at this stuff than you. You don't want to see or talk to him, but he doesn't mind."

I take a deep breath and consider lying to him. I could say that I don't mind either, or that Dave and I talk on the phone all the time. I could create a version of reality that might make him more comfortable. Or I could just blunder through with the truth.

"When your dad and I talk too much, it hurts because I have so many feelings right now. I'll need lots of time for my heart to get better."

He touches my hand in what has to be one of the most comforting, mature gestures a child has ever made. I kiss them all goodbye, head home with my carload of feelings, and put them all to bed, mentally ticking off another day, another unit of time.

"Where's your dad?" I ask when the kids come back from Dave's; he usually comes to the door and calls out hello. It's another way he's more polite than I am and another thing I've come to dread.

"He's getting married!" April says.

I look out the window, almost expecting to see Dave standing in front of his car in a tuxedo, maybe on his way to a black-tie event that April has spun into a fairy tale wedding.

But Logan throws his backpack on the floor and yells, "He's a jerk! I hate my idiot father. I wish he wasn't my dad."

Stunned, I look at Jed, who copies Logan by slamming down his own backpack, before wrapping his arms around my waist.

"Married? To Beth?" I say stupidly. I'm incredulous—the ink is barely dry on the divorce papers! Besides, I thought Dave didn't believe in monogamy.

"Uh-huh," April nods, unfazed.

I'm speechless—and outraged. My own father remarried three months after his divorce from my mother. His new wife had a daughter the same age as me and she moved into my bedroom with the green-and-yellow wallpaper I had chosen. She got a telephone put in that room and, presumably, was provided with heat and electricity and more than toast to eat. I stopped visiting my dad after that, so I'm not the best person to tell them that everything will be okay.

"That sucks," I say finally, because it does, and it's the best I can do.

I hear Logan crying in his bed several nights in a row after that. He says he's having nightmares about the world ending at the end of the year, when the Mayan calendar ends. He thinks the sun will burn out, and we'll all freeze to death.

"Mom, I'm so scared," he says, shivering. I climb into bed with him and pull the blanket up over our shoulders. I know the world won't end. It didn't end for me, at sixteen. But I know the feeling of watching things go up in flames and at the same time being so cold. I tuck the blanket close around him and hold on tight.

"No, I won't go!"

Jed is refusing to go to his karate class. It's a chilly autumn afternoon, and I'm holding his white cotton gi by the shoulders, hoping the sight of it will motivate him to put it on. I wave it a little, as if to say, *look! What a cool uniform this is!* He kicks and screams, saying he wants to quit.

I give up. "Fine, quit then."

He thrashes and shrieks, "I don't want to quit!" But he still won't go, so I tell him I'll take him to his friend Corey's house for a play date.

He quiets down enough to follow me out to the car, but when we pull up in front of his friend's house, he won't get out. He's changed his mind.

"Okay," I say, "we'll go home."

"No! I don't want to disappoint Corey." He sits there, not moving, looking tortured. Finally I drive away and he screams at me that I'm a jerk. At home, he goes into his bedroom to cry. I sit beside him and rub his back.

"This is a tough week," I say. "How are you feeling about your dad and Beth getting married?"

"I don't know!" he sobs.

"It's okay to be confused. Is there anything I can do to make things easier on you?"

"No karate," he mumbles.

"Okay, that's a deal. But you have to share your feelings, even if it's to say you don't know."

He cries harder. "I don't want to let Corey down."

"Oh, honey. You're not letting anyone down."

The next day, when I pick the kids up from their session with Sandy, their therapist, she pulls me aside and tells me that Dave asked Jed to walk Beth down the aisle at their wedding. Jed said no.

April hands me her worn copy of *The Little Mermaid* and climbs into my lap. She wants me to read it to her *again*, but I can't summon the enthusiasm. I'm disgusted with this story. The mermaid Ariel is willing to give up everything for Prince Eric, including her voice. Who writes this shit? I know that the original fairy tale was written by Hans Christian Andersen more than a century ago, but Walt Disney Pictures ruined it. The same Disney that took my daughter's first princess experience from me continues to corrupt her with this distorted view of romantic love. I want to fling the book across the room. Instead, I ask April if she's ready for the wedding. She becomes animated and talks for the next ten minutes about her new dress. For her, at least, the Magic Kingdom is still real.

"So here's what we're looking at." Scott hands me a piece of paper with two columns of figures on it. It's a breakdown of legal fees and payments. My stomach twists violently before I even see the numbers. I remind myself to breathe.

"As you know, you're entitled to half of Dave's retirement fund and that has already been dispersed. Your portion of nineteen thousand dollars will be applied to my balance and you'll owe a remaining five thousand. We can set up no-interest payments however you'd like."

"So I get nothing."

"There's no cash to split. It's all gone. But you've got the house and a good maintenance package. And Dave has a good job so your child support is significant."

I blink and stare at a large framed photo of a sand dune stretched before a blue horizon on the conference room wall. I have an eerily similar postcard pinned up at home of a sandy path disappearing into tall beach grass with the Henry David Thoreau quote, *Go confidently in the direction of your dreams. Live the life you've imagined!* I want to cry.

"Listen," Scott says. "I know it sucks. But you're going to be fine."

"What about the credit cards? Does he have to pay them off?"

"Here's what I recommend." He slides a business card across the table. It says Matt Gaffrey, Bankruptcy Attorney. "It'll give you a clean slate."

Looking at that word *bankruptcy* makes my eyes narrow. How can I attach my name to that? I want to yell, like Logan did, "I hate this!" I want to thrash and shriek, like Jed, "No, I won't do this!" I want to throw my own temper tantrum.

I take the card and manage a weak smile. I like Scott. I know he's done a good job for me. I also know that our relationship won't end with a check and handshake. Even with a divorce decree in my hand, I'll likely need him in my corner for an indefinite period of time.

We both stand and he puts a hand on my shoulder as we turn toward the door.

"Believe me, this divorce is worth every penny. You just don't know it yet."

I have a brief glimpse of the vision I had when the angel stretched out her arms and said, "All of this is yours." But nothing is mine.

I'm broke.

24 The Heart of the Matter

The loving and gentle parting I had hoped to orchestrate with Paul is not working. One night, watching television together, I mention to Paul that Dave and I once threw a party for the premiere of our favorite TV series.

"Guess what? Now he's doing the same thing with Beth."

Paul doesn't respond.

"They're even going on the same vacation with *my* old group of friends. It's like I was a piece of furniture he moved out and she's the new sofa that's put in the same spot and is supposed to look the same."

"Except newer," he says.

I cut my eyes at him. "Ouch."

He shrugs. "And they're not your friends anymore. They chose Dave."

I twist around on the sofa so I'm facing him. "What's wrong with you?"

He gives me a sullen look. "It seems obvious that you want him back."

I would laugh if this weren't so absurd. "How exactly is that obvious?"

"It just is. All your reminiscing about your parties and happy moments and vacations—"

"I mentioned one party!" Okay, I did mention more than that. "Am I allowed to have a memory?"

"Of course, but what's done is done. Why relive it?"

"I'm hardly reliving it."

"You're dwelling," he says scornfully. "To be honest, it's a little tiring seeing you sad all the time."

"Wow." I fall back against the sofa cushions. "That's so unfair. First of all, I'm sad *sometimes*, which is only natural after going through a *divorce*. It's far from all the time. And second of all, you're the one who looks sad."

"Why would I be sad?"

"That's what I'm asking."

"This has nothing to do with me." He reaches for the remote and switches off the TV, then hits the power button on the arm of his wheelchair and begins hoisting himself into it, which usually, at this time of night, signals that he's going to bed.

"End of discussion?"

He throws me an accusing look. "You're not the person you were."

"If you mean I'm not a puddle on the floor anymore, you're right!"

He shakes his head and turns his chair toward the bathroom. "You don't see it. And I'm really tired now, so I can't explain. Let's talk about it later."

I watch him roll into the bathroom and click the door shut. He's wrong. What I see, very clearly, is that he's happiest when I need his advice or adoration. He's not so comfortable when I remind him that I have interests outside of him, or when I start to resurrect any activity that came before him. But why does putting energy into myself mean I'm withdrawing it from him? Is there a limited supply? It's as if we're sharing a garden hose; one of us blooms while the other wilts, and then we switch.

Is it because Dave was so final, so brutal, that I'm afraid to be decisive? Would telling Paul it's over make me too much like Dave?

I can't bear the thought of being the one to cause pain, so Paul and I limp along. In an attempt to be modern and mature, we talk about being "friends with benefits," which is only prolonging the inevitable. We joke about this, as if it makes us strong when in fact we are cowardly and weak. Our "dates" dwindle to once a week at most and become tinged with quiet desperation. I reactivate my online dating profile and soon after, Paul, in the uncanny way that's become common between us, asks about it. I have to admit that yes, I'm officially putting myself out there. We agree that neither of us will sleep with anyone else without "giving notice."

I spend more of my free nights alone at home. Each time I drop the kids at Dave's apartment and don't go directly to Paul's, I experience a surge of near panic. If I break these evenings down—dinner in a Styrofoam container from Garcia's Mexican restaurant, a phone chat with my mom or a friend, an hour in front of the TV—I am able to find a routine that's bearable, but why is it so hard? What happened to the Tammy who went to London after college, alone, and found a job as a receptionist for three months? That girl was daring enough to go to a foreign country with nothing more than six hundred dollars in her pocket and an address for a place to find roommates. I can't imagine doing anything like that anymore.

I need to dare again. In my attempt to break free from Paul, I arrange a blind date. I meet a man named Jake at Northerly Island, and we walk along the lake beside the Adler Planetarium and the Field Museum. Jake is a widower, and I try to listen compassionately to his story, but I'm so nervous I can barely breathe. I feel trapped. I want to be with Paul. I can't be with Paul. I'm so frozen with indecision about the direction of my life that even this simple walk feels arduous.

When my date with Jake ends, I get in my car and check my phone. There are several texts from Paul reminding me that I promised to drop off a few of his things. I'm only blocks from his apartment. I text that I'll leave his things with his doorman.

"Come up?" he texts.

"If I can find parking," I text back, but I already know I'm going up. I circle the block until I see a car pulling away from the curb, then masterfully whip my Escape into the spot. I may not enjoy coming downtown, but at the very least it's made me an excellent parallel parker. I can fit myself into the most unlikely spaces. Paul's doorman, Leroy, buzzes me through the lobby and as I glide up to the twenty-ninth floor, I ask myself why I'm here. Isn't *because I want to be* a good enough reason? It certainly was for Dave.

I rap once on Paul's door and let myself in, knowing that he never locks it. I try not to think about *why* he leaves it open, so that if he falls either the doorman, or the building's maintenance engineer or, as has sometimes been the case, firefighters can get to him. I find him in a five o'clock shadow and a gray wool roll-neck sweater that makes him look like a Perry Ellis model. With an audible sigh, I sink onto the sofa beside him, feeling exhausted and relieved. He hands me a cold Bud Light, and we sit quietly sipping our beers. I have an overpowering urge to tell him about my date.

"So what were you up to tonight?" he asks, as if reading my mind.

I hesitate, not wanting to lie. "I went for a walk along the lake."

"Alone?" He's looking at me with a small, mysterious smile. I don't answer. "Because Steve sent me a text earlier. He saw you walking by the museum with a guy."

I stare at him. I can count the number of Paul's friends I've met on one hand, and one of them spotted me among the hundreds of people walking along the lakefront?

"I'm a big boy," Paul says, but I see the hurt on his face.

"It was a mistake." I look at him miserably, searching for words. "I was so nervous. . . ." I stop, aware that my nervousness doesn't justify running back to him or signify that I'm meant to be with him. I take a long swig of beer. I'm tempted to chug the whole thing, and I don't even like beer much.

"You're putting yourself out there," he says. "That's never easy."

I shoot him a grateful look. Then he adds, "And so am I."

"What's that mean?"

"I've been chatting with someone on Facebook. A girl I knew in junior high. She always had a crush on me."

So what? I nearly say. Obviously he's trying to insinuate something, but not for a moment do I believe that my position is threatened. When I don't answer, he squeezes my hand, turns my face toward him, and says quietly, "You know you're the only one I want."

I believe him. I also get the sense that I'm the only *thing* he wants and I feel a shadow of that trapped feeling I had earlier with Jake. What do *I* want? I still don't know. Paul's small apartment in the sky gets even smaller, like it's pushing me out. I put my beer down, move close to him, and we hold each other for a long time, not talking, bonded by a strange glue. It's a mix of misery and comfort, of return and goodbye. It's like trying to hold emptiness and wishing you could remember when it was something else.

The answer comes to me when I'm standing at the stove watching a pot of water, waiting for it to boil so I can make spaghetti for dinner: I want to write books. That's it. Just those five words. And they're not even new words. They've been stamped in my consciousness since I was a little girl, put there by some other hand, since I have no recollection of formulating such a specific desire on my own. But instead of being comforted by how strong and simple my purpose is, anxiety breaks through the surface like the bubbles breaking through the water. It's not enough. If it were enough, why would I keep forgetting and veering off course? Why would I keep putting it—forgive the pun—on the back burner?

Paul said I'm putting myself out there. Am I? Maybe by going on a date. But what about efforts that aren't attached to a man? What am I doing just for me? I want to be selfish. Not to explain anything to anyone—least of all Dave—but to tell my story and allow the pages to be the witness I've always craved.

The timer chimes. I turn off the flame, protect my hand with an oven mitt before grabbing the pot, and then upend it over a strainer in the sink. The steam blasts me in the face and I blink. Then I run cool water over the noodles and imagine this: I am my own witness. To my own life. I have a story. And it belongs to me. I repeat this over and over while I set the table, divide the spaghetti onto four plates, and call the kids to come eat.

It's the third day of what I've decided will be my new routine: drop the kids at school, home by nine a.m., meditate, make a cup of tea, write for at least fifty minutes, take a ten minute break, repeat. I'm in the middle of this regiment when my cell phone rings; I forgot to turn it off—a rookie mistake. Paul's name appears. I should ignore it, but it's been ten days since we've seen each other. It's the longest we've been apart since we started dating.

I answer. When he responds his voice sounds strange.

"Do you have a cold?" I ask.

With no warning, he blurts it out: *I slept with her.*

The translation happens instantly: Slept = sex. Her = junior high friend. It hits me in the gut. Unlike the numbing shock I felt with Dave that seemed to separate my head from my body, this is a blast of nausea and pain that makes me grab my stomach. And instead of sinking to the floor, I jump up and turn in jerks around the room, wailing like a lost child. "This is not what we agreed! This is not what I wanted!"

He keeps repeating, "I had to tell you. I had to tell you," while

I continue to cry. Finally he says, "I'm sorry," and I see something else: Walter was right. The word sorry is meaningless. But what did I expect? I've been pushing and pulling him for months. By sleeping with someone else, Paul did the one thing he knew I couldn't overlook.

The horse has bucked us off.

I spend the next week flat on my sofa watching every episode of the BBC show *Doc Martin*. I don't know why I'm so comforted by this show, which is about the unlikely love affair between a brusque doctor and a beautiful school teacher; a doctor who, by the way, doesn't even try to express his feelings and doesn't give a damn if that makes people uncomfortable. You would think I'd hate it, but from the opening shot, when the music starts and the camera pans over the picturesque seaside harbor, I'm transported to the English countryside. I forget that I'm shattered and alone in Chicago. Maybe it brings me back to my twenty-something self, venturing toward an unknown adventure an ocean away. I might have had a different life if I had made different choices. I might have snagged an English husband, like one of my roommates did. Instead of returning home to find a job in marketing that I would eventually hate, I could be living in London with the ginger-haired boy named Angus who flirted with me and took me to visit his parents in Devonshire, where they lived on a family estate so large that half the house was not used. But at twenty-one, my life script did not read like a romantic comedy. I was too responsible to romp, so here I am, twenty years later, alone on my sofa, inexplicably enchanted, once again, by a churlish, emotionally unavailable doctor on a TV show.

Every few hours my phone starts to buzz. Paul texts in bursts, followed, eventually, by long silences when I don't respond. His messages range from polite friendliness to this confusing confession: *I love you more than you can imagine. I don't see this breakup as being forever. I see us back together, better for each other.*

I turn my phone on mute and try to meditate. I can't do it, so I force myself outside. With slow, iron-limbed steps I walk to the park near my house, collapse under the weeping willow tree, and call my older brother Bryan.

"No matter what I do, I get tossed aside," I cry. "And everyone else finds love so easily!" I try to keep my weeping silent, like the tree, because I'm in a public place and, though there's no one passing by at the moment, that could quickly change. My voice rises anyway. "Everyone is so fucking dishonest. Why do people say one thing and do another?"

Then, as if moved by a gust of wind, I twirl into anger. "And *fuck* Paul for fucking with my writing time! Goddamn it! Why do these asshole men insist on dropping bombs when I'm trying to write? That really pisses me off." And on and on I blow and bend and rustle and rail while Bryan listens. He has no idea what to say to me but it doesn't matter because he also has no choice but to listen. He's my brother. He sees me at my worst. And he can't leave.

It's a Friday night, and the kids are with me. Though I consider myself to be a creative and resourceful person, I draw a blank when it comes to thinking of fun weekend activities to do with them. In the middle of my guilt trip, Bryan calls to tell me that our dad is back in the hospital. His valve replacement surgery bought him some time, but his heart is still the size of a volleyball and growing weaker. It's too late for him to get a heart transplant, but the doctors are going to insert a ventricular assist device, or mechanical pump, that could add a few years to his life. Everything looks good for the surgery. Then, hours before it's scheduled, he develops an infection. The surgery is postponed. By the time Bryan arrives at the hospital two days later, my dad has developed pneumonia and is unconscious.

"He's been transferred to palliative care," Bryan says.

I keep my phone in my pocket, waiting for updates. It's been eight days since Paul texted that he saw us back together someday, better for each other. I feel worse, not better, but I don't want to go through this alone. I text him that my dad is dying; he doesn't reply. I know he's attending a multiple sclerosis conference in the suburbs. Months ago, he invited me, but I'm certain he brought his "old friend" instead. They're probably in the hotel room now, ordering room service and reminiscing about their mutual fifth grade crush while his phone vibrates, unnoticed, in the pocket of the pants that are in a ball on the floor. I hate that I'm thinking of this instead of focusing on my dad, but I can't force feelings I "should" be having about a father I never really had.

My dad doesn't wake up. He dies of congestive heart failure early Monday morning. He had just turned seventy. It was the milestone he was aiming for, but didn't expect to reach. I text Paul again: *My dad died.* He doesn't answer.

When he finally calls two days after my dad's death, I say, "I missed you terribly and really needed to talk to you."

"You can always talk to me." It's a lie and we both know it. His refrain for so long was "I'm your go-to guy," but those were just more hollow words. He won't acknowledge the death of us, and blithely ignores the fact that he's sleeping with someone else. I vow to myself that I won't talk to him again. I don't need him. I don't need anyone. But each morning, as soon as I open my eyes and before I can move another muscle, it's as if someone sets a flat weight about a foot wide on my chest. It stays on me all day, pressing, pressing, making me feel trapped and increasingly desperate. One thought circles my brain like a gerbil: Paul said he loves me.

More than you can imagine. Those were his words. I've reread them on my phone at least fifty times.

Suddenly Paul's love becomes something I *must* have or I'll die. Why didn't I see it before? Why was I so stingy with him? I can't let him go. I just can't.

I have to explain myself. I have to make Paul understand me. So I turn to the surest way I know to make sense of this: paper and pen. I write him a letter. I flatter, I bargain, I rewrite. I promise him that I can be better—more lovable, more appreciative, less focused on the past. I find reasons for my waffling: I was scared, I was selfish, I was wrong. I never mention the other woman.

I hate myself for writing this instead of something, *anything* else—a blog, a chapter, a journal entry—for myself. I hate that after all I've been through, I'm still begging for love. I'm a fucking cliché. Mostly I resent having to feel brokenheartedness to such an extreme that I can't even begin to describe it. Because not being able to describe something, not being able to make sense of it on a page, that's the most complete desolation I know. To be left is painful, but to be left with no voice is unbearable.

I put the letter in an envelope, stamp and address it to Paul, and tuck it into my purse with my electric bill. After dropping the kids at school, I swing by the post office and drop both envelopes in the box, pretending that this is just business as usual, pretending that I'm a mature, self-aware woman reasonably expressing herself rather than a hopeless, disillusioned romantic grasping at straws.

Then I wait, heavy with the fear that I'll never love or trust again, and paralyzed by the certainty that life will never get any easier. The weekend comes; I gather my kids around me on the sofa and let them watch hour after hour of whatever TV shows they want, even Disney shows. Against the sound of their bickering, I close my eyes and watch different, forgotten images: my dad's back as he stands straddling a snowmobile, trying to stay on a trail that winds into darkness, a triangle of yellow from the headlight cutting out the only safe shape. The engine is loud. The forest is quiet. The air smells like gas. My brother sits beside me in the sleigh, both of us bundled in snowsuits with a blanket over our knees. My nose is frozen. When I open my eyes, the four of us are still here, sitting on the sofa. We are the four ventricles of a still-beating heart, but we are swollen with grief. My nose drips. The kids are quiet now, drifting into sleep. I look at my phone, knowing there is no blinking light. I compose a new text, the same text: *My dad died.* But I don't send it to anyone. I just look at the words until my phone goes black in my hand.

25 A Belief in Beauty

I lie awake night after night, dying for a touch. It's a physical ache that has me tossing and turning and reaching back in time to the last loving touch Dave and I shared. It was Thanksgiving weekend, in his parents' basement, where a bed is set up in the back corner of their TV room. It was very late that Friday night, four days before he called me to our table and turned my world upside down. I slept while he watched movies upstairs with his brothers. I remember kissing him when he finally came downstairs and climbed under the covers. It was unusual for me to feel amorous when my coveted sleep was interrupted, but that night I did, and I remember Dave seemed surprised. And hesitant. Had some part of me known that would be our last kiss, our last embrace? Was my body acting on its own to store away his touch, his smell, his sounds—sensations that, however faded they may have become after twenty years, would soon be gone?

And if I had actually known that would be the last time, how might it have been different? Would I have been able to close at least one of the doors of my heart more gently?

Then, of course, my thoughts turn to Paul, specifically his hands. Though he wasn't able to move his left hand, his right hand was strong and broad; holding it and feeling the surprising strength of it clasping mine is arguably my favorite memory of him. The absence of that touch wrenches some decades-old glacier of loneliness in me that now feels more firmly fixed than ever.

As if to demonstrate an uncanny radar, my phone buzzes on the nightstand, glowing with Paul's name. My heart leaps before I even read the text.

Come over.

I wait, expecting more, something along the lines of *your letter has rocked my world and we need to talk.*

But the phone sits silently in my palm, stubborn and uncooperative. Should I text back? Or better, call and ask him to clarify? He admitted to me once that he dreads saying the wrong thing over the phone, that unless he can look in my eyes or hold my hand, he gets scared; it was a confession I found vulnerable and sweet.

But I've also been vulnerable. And I don't especially like being ordered up like the special of the day. I deliberately set the phone back on the nightstand and corral my thoughts.

How grateful I am that I'm learning to be alone and that I'm no longer afraid of my feelings! How grateful I am that I'm learning to express myself! I don't care how lonely being alone can feel; I will not be anyone's sloppy seconds. I've weathered the storm. I survived a divorce. There's so much Paul doesn't know about the *real* me, so much he never knew.

And yet, I keenly recall all the times he listened to me and encouraged me. I remember his disarming smile and the way he would cut through my confusion with the words, "If you love me, say you love me." Why can't it be that easy?

The phone buzzes again and I reach for it.

Come over. Please?

He knows my schedule and that the kids are at Dave's tonight. How persistent will he be?

I sit up, turn on the light, and reach for the book of poems on my bedside table. I open to Amy Lowell:

The world is full of rude awakenings
and heaven-born castles shattered to the ground
yet still our human longing vainly clings
to a belief in beauty through all wrongs.

Yes. My human longing is in full cling mode. Because I *do* believe in beauty. Despite everything, I believe in happy endings. In a world of rude awakenings, wouldn't it be wonderful if love could come down to two simple words? *Come over.*

I have to go. I change from pajamas to sweatpants and a sweatshirt, brush my teeth, and grab my purse. Before my car has left the garage, I sense the regret that will await my return, and as my headlights slice the night sky, I explain myself to the darkness: *I have a heart connection with Paul unlike anything I've ever felt, and I have to see him once more just to see. . . .* What? I don't know, but it doesn't matter. What matters is that I'm stronger now, and wiser.

It's cold in the car. I rushed out without my coat and my teeth are chattering. At this time, after midnight, Lake Shore Drive is deserted and I make it downtown in fifteen minutes, but even this feels tortuously slow. My teeth continue to chatter in the elevator. When I let myself into Paul's apartment, I find him on his sofa in his usual spot and could easily fool myself into believing these last couple of weeks apart never happened. His smile is as true as ever, and the light in his eyes immediately warms me. We fall into each other, and for a few moments I experience safety and relief. I knew my letter would illuminate the truth between us! I want to ask him about it, but he doesn't want to talk. The happy ending I envision is different from the one he desires, and I feel a hollowness growing in my chest as I realize that I won't find my heaven-born castle in his twenty-ninth floor apartment.

"You got my letter," I finally manage to say. It's not a question.

"That was so sweet of you," he says, barely looking at me before burying his head in my neck.

My face flushes, fired not by his touch but by a sudden, acute stab of embarrassment. I'm ridiculous. Another woman has been here, on this sofa, drinking in Paul's face, appreciating Paul's hands, and either ignorant of my existence or laughing at my foolish desperation. I can picture her here in the room with us in a way I could never picture any of the women Dave was with.

"I have to go," I say, and when Paul doesn't protest, I stumble to my feet. I leave more confused, more sad, more alone, and something else—ashamed. I'm not strong. I'm weak, and in my weakness I think of Dave. When have I ever experienced real temptation? Now, still reeling from the taste of it, I see that I can't control myself any better than Dave could control himself. At the same time, we're both controlling. I want to control whether or not someone is allowed to leave me. During one of our arguments, Paul once said, "You have a script that I have to follow."

He was right.

Perhaps it's not possible to outrun humiliation, but it doesn't hurt to try.

I escape with my kids to Michigan, where I've arranged a weekend home exchange. Instead of enjoying a pleasant getaway, I feel like I'm running from more hurt and betrayal. Paul continues to text me but his messages are infuriatingly inane. He knew I had this weekend planned so he sends annoying, random pieces of information like the traffic patterns on I-94 or the weather forecast for Southwest Michigan.

Ignoring him, I force myself to relax and enjoy this time away with my kids, even as I recognize that forcing and relaxing are the ultimate foes. It is fun to pull into the circular gravel driveway in front of our getaway house, which is a stunning contemporary ranch framed by a stand of white birch trees in front and an apron of pine trees in back, with a porch that curves around the whole place like a smile. I locate the keys inside a garage that looks like the storeroom of a sporting goods store and we let ourselves into a five-bedroom, toy-and-gadget-filled playground that's ours for two days. The kids rush straight to the massive flat screen TV and gaming system, while I take in the vaulted ceilings, the tasteful French Country decor, and the expansive view outside a wall of sliding glass doors. I notice several painted barn-wood wall hangings that declare the essence of this family:

As for me and my house, we will serve the Lord.

He is before all things. And in Him all things hold together.

In the kitchen, my heart leaps at the sight of a high-end European espresso maker. Right now, for me, coffee is before all things, so I make myself a cup before exploring the rest of the house. The stairway to the second floor is like the hall of a gallery, exhibiting perfectly-placed pieces of a storybook wedding and perfect family. The master bathroom is bigger than my bedroom in the city. There's a whirlpool tub surrounded by creamy marble and a shower with steam sauna. The bed is a king-sized cloud of white goose down that I admire with a mix of awe and wariness, knowing that once I'm in it, I may never leave.

Back on the first floor, I sink into a gorgeous camel-colored arm-chair and sigh. I hope this family is as pleased with our house, which can't compare to this one in terms of creature comforts but at least boasts some value in location and the dubious charm of urban grit. I tell myself that it's a fair trade.

Yet, as I sit back and sip my coffee, I feel heavier, not lighter. Here I am, a single mom with three kids. No husband. No boyfriend. I don't know what we're doing here, playing house in a strange place, pretending to be what we're not. I begin to feel that this absent family is watching us. I can't turn my head without seeing one of their precious moments. But there are no candid shots. They're all posed, and the husband could be a cardboard cut-out; he's magazine handsome and looks exactly the same in each picture. I judge the wife as a woman who needs reminders at every turn: We're married! I was skinny! You made promises! I look again at the Bible verses adorning the walls. Why does everything have to be such a declaration?

Being here makes me hate marriage. Or maybe I just hate Dave's impending marriage to Beth. With the kids in the basement happily rifling through other people's toys and no housework to pull me into busyness, I let myself think about Dave and Beth. I try to picture them in love, married, living together. What will they have that we didn't? Will Dave cheat on her too? I probe these thoughts like a tongue that keeps touching a canker sore, searching for the ache, but I don't feel much pain. Am I in denial? Maybe, unwittingly, I'm back to my old habit of stuffing my feelings into a capsule that will whizz through a scaffold and pop out somewhere down the road, just when I'm starting to develop my own picture of happiness. Should I feel more, and if I don't, does that mean I'm emotionally damaged?

When the kids come up for dinner, I stop trying to gauge my feelings and ask about theirs.

"So guys," I say brightly. "How's everything going at your dad's? Are you looking forward to Beth moving in with you?"

"Beth made Daddy a book of our artwork for his birthday gift," April says. My smile sticks to my face, masking my urge to groan.

"Yeah," Logan adds, "And then she had to have a private talk with us because we didn't give Dad any birthday gifts." He rolls his eyes.

"She did *what*?"

"She said Daddy's feelings were hurt and told us to make him belated cards," Jed says.

Heat rushes to my face. Maybe it's the caffeine, or maybe it's simply a straightforward, unstuffed, justifiable emotion. Private talks with the kids about their dad are *my* job. Never mind the voice of recrimination whispering that this could have been avoided if I'd helped the kids buy birthday gifts for Dave. I didn't want to think about his birthday. Maybe it was stingy and selfish, but that's not the point.

"So did you? Make cards?"

"I did," April and Jed say in unison.

"I didn't," says Logan. This is probably a good time for me to deliver a loving message about honoring thy father, but I don't feel qualified at the moment. Besides, I don't want to lose my indignation and the power it has to propel me into action. While the kids finish their tacos, I push my plate away and whip off an ominous text to Dave informing him that all of us—he, Beth, and I—will be meeting with the kids' therapist to discuss the role Beth will play with the kids once they're married. I'm not asking. I'm *declaring*. Dave responds agreeably, and his unexpected compliance, instead of putting me at ease, further unnerves me. I've spent months trying to anticipate and understand when he'll choose to be combative and it's been impossible to establish a pattern. Our time as a family, if put into candid shots, would be all over the place. Maybe that's why I dislike the perfectly arranged wall of family photos in this house, because I don't have any orderly, predictable snapshots to anchor me. I haven't earned the right to stencil my wall with the flowing calligraphy in this couple's bedroom, words I missed the first time I was in there but that seem to glow in the darkness as I try to fall asleep later that night:

> *Be devoted to one another in love. Honor one another above yourselves. Romans 12:10*

I want to argue with that one. It's a nice idea, but isn't it time for me to honor myself, to put myself first? That doesn't mean I won't devote myself to my children and stand up for what I feel is right for them, but where does Dave fit into this idea of devotion? Now that our family is shattered, what creed will we follow? What values will guide our way? I think again of the quote downstairs—*in Him all things hold together*—and have to admit that all of this, from the photos and faith on the walls, to the view from their window, to the five pairs of skis lined up in the garage, it's all beautiful. And that makes me incredibly sad.

That night, I leave the window cracked and climb into the downy softness of a stranger's king-size bed, enjoying the faint scent of Michigan pine that wafts in on the breeze. I'm about to drift into sleep when my cell phone buzzes.

It's a text from Paul. I open it to see a naked selfie of him. Is it a joke? Is it meant for his new girlfriend? Or is he only being cruel?

Did you mean to send me this? I text. The clock beside the bed reads 10:30 p.m. I watch as it ticks on. Twenty minutes go by. Thirty minutes. It's past eleven when it buzzes again.

I don't know how that happened, he responds. *It's an old photo and I must have forwarded it by accident. I can't believe you think I would intentionally send that.*

I almost fall for it and jump to the conclusion that my thinking is off. For a split second I'm the woman I've always been, the one who doubts herself and is ashamed of thinking ill thoughts toward anyone, the one who isn't supporting, loving, or forgiving enough. As I look at his words—*I can't believe you think*—they strike me as very familiar. How many times has Dave said practically the same thing? *I can't believe you did that*, or *I can't believe you think that*. Am I really so unbelievable? I do what Abigail calls a "reality check." Am I crazy, drunk, or high? Do other people seem confused by me? The answer to both questions is no. NO. It reverberates within me with the sound of a million clanging gongs, and something old and small and scared falls away. I shared my heart with Paul, and the only response comes in the form of a sext. Talk about stripping things down. I delete the naked picture, along with Paul's contact information. I've carved out one too many pieces of my heart and delivered them, wrapped in paper and imploring words, to undeserving men. The quest for love, understanding, respect, or honesty has always been a battle, and it has never been a fair fight because my white flag was already raised, obscuring my face, my voice, my Self. Now, it's a choice between that woman or the real me, the one I know I can be.

I choose me.

26 Matthew 17:20

Monday morning dawns bright and clear, making it easier to return to our Chicago routine. We tried on another family's life in Michigan, but now it's time to get back to our own. After dropping the kids off at school, I struggle through the back door, my arms laden with bags of groceries. I set them down on the kitchen counter and stop, listening. Something is different in the house. It's not a noise. What I hear is more of an emptiness, a vacant feeling. I walk through the rooms trying to pinpoint the change and the detached, slightly surreal feeling it's giving me. Is it the natural after effects of being away, in a bigger, brighter, nicer house? Or has my old companion, loneliness, sneaked in to wait for me?

I put the cereal, peanut butter, bread, and cans of soup haphazardly on the pantry shelves, not bothered that my food storage has devolved into disorganization. I stand in the middle of the kitchen and look at the pressed wood cabinets that could use another coat of paint and the refrigerator that thrums and vibrates in a march toward death and think of my recent victory march over being awarded this house. Suddenly some facts appear before me, almost as if they're printed on the grocery receipt there on the counter: the real estate market is in a slump, which means that I'm not sitting on a valuable asset. As long as the mortgage can't be refinanced, the property title will bind me to Dave, and that's a situation that could stretch on for years. I see these things clearly, without emotion, and recognize that my house has let me go. My affection for my hundred-year-old Victorian friend is still present, but it's different. I'm reminded of the moment when I knew it was time to tell the kids about our divorce, the way that decision struck like a thunderclap. This morning there is no thunder. What I sense is more of a gentle sigh, as if some spirit has moved on.

I get my journal from my bedroom and sit at the dining room table. Opening to a blank page, I write: *Where do I want to live? What would I like?* I don't write what would I like to *change?* Or what would I like to *improve?* Or what should I *do?* I just write what would I like? Full stop. The shorter sentence reaches so much farther into possibility.

A list emerges: a first-floor apartment with three bedrooms, an updated kitchen, a bright sunny space, a view onto a backyard, a garage, in a better neighborhood, near shops or cafes, closer to the lake.

Before I can overthink what I'm doing, I make an appointment with a rental agent for the following week, then resolve to put it out of my mind. I spend a little time that afternoon reading a book called *The Divine Matrix.* The author, Gregg Braden, writes about how the faith of a mustard seed can move a mountain. He refers to Matthew 17:20, which says, "If your faith is the size of a mustard seed you will say to this mountain 'Move from here to there,' and it will move; nothing will be impossible for you."

When the kids get home from school, April plops down beside me with her backpack. She pulls out a book by Arnold Lobel called *Ming Lo Moves the Mountain.* I get goose bumps. At five, she's an excellent reader, and I might wonder if what she "reads" is actually memorized, except that I've never seen this book. She begins, "I want to move the mountain that is near my house." With me helping her sound out new words, we finish the story together: Ming Lo tries running into the mountain with a tree trunk. He tries making noise with pots and pans, and baking cakes for the mountain. Nothing works. Then a wise man teaches him to step to "the dance of the moving mountain," which looks exactly like walking backwards. They pack up their things, put their bundles on their backs, and do the "dance." The mountain moves!

"There was happiness in their hearts for they both knew that they had made the mountain move," reads April. We put the book away, and after dinner and a bath, April giggles as she walks backward from the bathroom to her bedroom, saying, "Look! I'm dancing!" I tuck first her and then the boys into bed, then crawl into my own bed where I can wrap myself around this wonderful idea, that what feels like moving backwards might actually be moving us forward.

Determined to keep moving forward, I enroll in an eight-week "deepening" class at my spiritual center; through meditation, journaling, and group exercises, we dive into our pain and fears and learn to apply spiritual truths. We're asked to ponder these questions: What needs to be on the line for me to show up and participate in my life? What's on the line if I don't?

If I think of my faith as a plant, I would expect it to be in full bloom. I believe that my journey with Dave has made me a careful gardener; I've diligently watered my spirituality. What I realize in this class is that the roots of my faith are shallow, just like a plant that is too often drenched by a hovering, over eager hand. Each week when the group meets I feel close to losing it, though I'm not sure what that would mean. Embarrassment? Public humiliation? I don't want to find out.

One morning, we begin a walking meditation. The question we

are given to bring to God is, "What do I need to do to know you more?" The teacher reminds us to honor one another by not interfering in anyone else's experience. That means we do not speak or offer comfort. We allow a safe space for all emotions. Head down, I begin circling the room, silently repeating, "What do I need to do. . .? What do I need to do. . .?" The answer is immediate: stop being afraid. But even this thought frightens me. I can rail against my fears, I can ram them with reason, or push against them with brave actions, and they won't move. No matter what I do, I can't let go of the sense that, if I'm not on guard, if I don't keep it together, something terrible will happen. Surrendering to God feels like losing control, and losing control looks like . . . what? I don't even dare to imagine.

In Arnold Lobel's children's book, the wise man tells Ming Lo to take his house apart, stick by stick, then bundle it together with all his possessions, face the mountain, and close his eyes.

He says, "You will put your left foot in a place that is in back of your right foot. Then you will put your right foot in a place that is in back of your left foot. You must do this again and again for many hours. When you open your eyes, you will see that the mountain has moved far away."

I want so badly for this fear to move! I'm ready to enjoy peace in my house, but I don't know how to achieve it. As I circle the room, head down, emotion rises in me like a tidal wave. I fall to my knees, put my head on a chair, and cry. I'm in a roomful of people, finally "losing it." But nothing terrible happens. No one laughs or judges me. After a few minutes I get up and blow my nose. I finish the class and, putting one foot in front of the other, I go home.

27 A Stream of Events

Martin is an astrologer who sits outside his apartment in a small tourist town in Michigan next to a sandwich board that advertises his readings. The first time I had a session with him was something of a lark. I don't know much about astrology and had never had my star chart mapped out. He charmed me, not only with his accurate summaries of my personality and history, but with his own story. He had played violin with the Chicago Symphony Orchestra until his passion for music was replaced by a love of the stars. Now in his late sixties, he lives a quiet, nearly monastic life in a small room just off the main street of this idyllic summertime town, where he watches hundreds of movies on his VCR when he isn't giving readings at the table that takes up his entire living space.

The last time I saw Martin he was recovering from a stroke. It affected his speech and had to be affecting his business. But I was able to understand him enough to hear the messages he saw spelled out for me in the stars. He didn't—couldn't —mince words.

"Don't give your power to any judge or lawyer," he said. "Make the decisions that are best for you and your kids and don't ask permission."

He gave me a poem that is most commonly attributed to the philosopher Goethe and told me to study it and live by it:

Until one is committed, there is hesitancy, the chance to draw back—concerning all acts of initiative (and creation), there is one elementary truth the ignorance of which kills countless ideas and splendid plans: that the moment one definitely commits oneself, then Providence moves too. All sorts of things occur to help one that would never otherwise have occurred. A whole stream of events issues from the decision, raising in one's favor all manner of unforeseen incidents and meetings and material assistance, which no man could have dreamed would have come his way. Whatever you can do, or dream you can do, begin it. Boldness has genius, power, and magic in it. Begin it now.

I'm thinking of Martin as I stand on the sidewalk outside a small rental house just two miles from my house. What would he think of my idea to move? Is this the boldness he advised? Mostly I feel hesitant and tell myself that I have every chance to draw back. No decision has been made.

When the rental agent arrives—a wiry, serious young man wearing a navy pork pie hat—I shake his hand and take out the list I made in my journal. I like the possibility of living in a single-family home, with no rental units upstairs, but this one, despite its cute cottage-like feel, is too small to be practical. There is barely space for a full-sized sofa in the front room. Undaunted, we head to the next address, the first floor of a brick three-flat that sits on a corner lot in a clean, quiet neighborhood closer to Lake Michigan.

What I notice first when the rental agent opens the front door are the two columns that flank the living room and separate it from the dining room, then the crown molding—both decorative touches that weren't on my list, but instantly delight me. So do the large windows on the front and the side that let in generous swatches of sunlight. It's a typical Chicago floor plan, with the combined living and dining rooms in front, the bedrooms off the hallway, and the kitchen in the back. As I follow the agent across the deep reddish-brown hardwood floors, I feel excitement begin to ripple through me. Stepping into the kitchen is like stepping in front of a wave and feeling the thrill of being lifted off your feet. What would ordinarily be a smallish room adjoining an enclosed but uninsulated back porch has been reno-vated so that the kitchen flows into a sunroom and allows a sweeping view of the backyard. Instantly I know I'll be living here. I see myself writing in this back room, just there by the window, with a view of a bird feeder and the sidewalk with its slow but steady stream of pass-ersby to keep loneliness at bay. It's also a perfect space for healing sessions, with room for a massage table and a door that leads outside.

The agent points out the upgrades in the kitchen, adding that the previous owners lived for a long time in this unit and put in features that the second and third floor apartments don't have. I don't even need to consult my list. This apartment has everything I wrote down and more, including private access from the hallway to a massive unfinished basement that could store an arsenal of Nerf guns and a battalion of Barbie dolls. In the few minutes it takes to step out the back to see the landscaped yard and garage, I'm already wondering if I should blurt out that I'll take it or try to play it cool.

I attempt to do both. "I'm ready to sign a lease," I say, as offhand-edly as possible. Maybe the agent was trying to play it cool as well, because now, in a burst of enthusiasm, he tells me what a gem I've found, and I don't bother pointing out that *he* found it because it's obvious he's already proud of himself.

I wake up at four in the morning thinking about the apartment. Aside from meeting Paul, I can't remember the last time I felt so giddy and hopeful, so pulled forward by a clear, bright beam, without clouds of uncertainty or the gray pall of divorce dimming the light. I lie awake planning the furniture I'll need and where each piece will go. I want to simplify, and vow to leave behind anything that's beat up, threadbare, or outdated. Everything I pack will have to earn its place in my new home, either by its necessity or beauty. There will be no room in my life for sentimentality. The idea of living this way calls to me as an accomplishment and a fresh start.

I must fall back asleep, because the next thing I know, it's past seven and I need to rush to get the kids out of bed. I won't say anything to them about moving, not yet. In the pale morning light, the news churns inside me. I butter a piece of toast and chew it slowly while the kids pour themselves bowls of Cheerios and sit at the table. Jed looks sullen and tired, Logan opens a Captain Underpants book, and April chatters brightly about the hamster in Miss Emily's room and how it will only eat the long carrots and not the baby ones from a plastic bag, and how Miss Emily says that's okay, he shouldn't have too many carrots anyway because they have too much sugar in them, and isn't that crazy because carrots are *vegetables*, not sugar! I nod, only half listening, considering my next step. I won't be able to keep it a secret from Dave or Scott for long.

After dropping off the kids, I spend time in the backyard deadheading the petunias, which, despite looking leggy and wan, are valiantly crossing into autumn. When I can't find another dead bloom to pinch, I wipe my hands off on my jeans, take out my cell phone, and call Scott. He answers after one ring.

"What's up?"

"Well, I'm realizing that I'm not going to be able to afford this house over the long term."

"I told you we'll petition to increase your support."

"Yes, but you also said our next court date has been pushed back two months." I focus on keeping my voice light and even. "So, I looked at a couple of apartments and I found one I like. The kids and I are going to move."

"That is not an option for you. You said you wanted the house."

I look up at the sloped roof and the squat brick chimney that needs tuck-pointing, just one of the many unexpected repairs included in homeownership. "I know, but—"

"Let me explain this to you. The judge has awarded you the house. It's entered in a court order, so you could be held in contempt if you move. And remember, you don't have sole custody, so you can't do it without informing Dave."

"Obviously I'll inform him. And this could work out very well for him. He doesn't have a long term lease where he is now."

"If he moves back into the house, he could argue that he's the more stable parent."

"Come on, Scott!" I lower my voice and walk around to the side of the house, realizing that my neighbor may have her bedroom window cracked. "Think about it. He has options here. He's the only one who can refinance or modify the loan, but the mortgage needs to be in arrears for that to happen. If I skip a payment, it could work in his favor. Or he could let it go into foreclosure and bank some money in the meantime."

"The judge could order you to move back in."

I think about a lesson from *A Course in Miracles* that says, "I am under no law but God's." I'm tempted to say this to Scott. Instead, I say, "It's done. I've signed a lease and I'm moving. It's your job to make it work." It comes out more forcefully than I intend.

I hear him exhale. "We have to go about it the right way. I don't want to destroy the goodwill we've built with the judge."

"You can start by pointing out that I'm the only one cutting expenses here. This is the best decision for me and my kids and it makes sense financially for all of us."

"Okay, I'll file an emergency motion."

I hear a clicking sound, like he's rapping his pen against his desk. I wait.

"I like it!" he says finally, cheerfully. As if it was his idea all along.

28 Hear Me Roar

I don't want to be cocky, but as I lean toward the mirror in the bathroom outside the kids' therapist's office, I feel excessively proud of myself. My story began with being called to the table, then falling to the floor, followed by a long-running game of musical chairs in which I faced lawyers, a judge, several therapists, a mediator, Ron the job "expert," Dr. Smith, and now, Beth. On that night, that unforgettable night, Dave told me I needed to be *resilient*. He was right.

I carefully apply my new lipstick, give myself an encouraging smile, and reach for the door. Dave and Beth have just arrived. I've met Beth once before, briefly, when I dropped the kids at Dave's. We exchange polite hellos before Sandy ushers us into her room.

Sandy has been seeing Logan, Jed, and April for several months, both individually and as part of a support group for children of divorce, and all of us, Dave included, like her very much. Jed, my mysterious, self-contained middle child, actually throws himself at her legs whenever he sees her. Her room has shelves of games and toys and a small round table. We arrange ourselves awkwardly around it, sitting on chairs that are meant for children. After Sandy makes us comfortable and invites us to share, I ask Beth questions like, "Will you be picking the kids up from school? Should I coordinate things with you while Dave is at work? What are your concerns about step-parenting?" Each time Beth looks to Dave before answering, but he doesn't say much, leaving her to fumble her way through topics they obviously haven't discussed. Finally I bring up Dave's birthday and how Beth admonished the kids for not giving him cards.

Taking a deep breath, I say, "My kids are not responsible for their father's feelings. If he has an issue with them, he can talk to them about it. I don't want you negotiating their relationship. It's none of your business."

Beth looks at me a moment, her eyes wide beneath raised brows, then starts to cry.

"I'm so sorry," she says, and I have to check my instinct to say it's okay or make it easier on her. Clearly she's been thrown into the deep end, and Dave is not exactly tossing her a lifeline. But I refuse to make that my problem. Maybe I'm being mean, but I'm starting to think *mean* gets a bad rap. Is a mother bear mean? Or is she acting naturally?

I study my hands, hoping to give Beth a moment. Then, because I don't think things could possibly get more uncomfortable, I forge ahead with the other piece of news I've been waiting to share. I look at Dave and force my voice to remain steady.

"Since we're all here, it's probably a good time to let you know that I've rented an apartment and the kids and I will be moving in three weeks."

His eyes narrow. He looks at Sandy, as if she was in on this and he's deciding whether to chastise her or respond to me. But Sandy looks at me as well, clearly waiting for more.

"And it's not up for discussion," I quickly add. "It's done." I'm calmer this time, even when he starts to sputter that this is impossible, just impossible! In fact, the word makes me smile.

"Nothing is impossible. The word itself says 'I'm possible.'" I'm attempting to be humorous by quoting Audrey Hepburn, one of my favorite actresses, but no one seems to catch this.

"I can't believe you did this!" He uses that tight voice that makes me steel myself. I'm glad Sandy and Beth are present to keep this civil.

"Look at the bright side. You now have a house all to yourself." I gesture to include Beth. "You can sell it—"

"It's under water!"

"—or stop paying rent and let it go into foreclosure."

"I don't want that on my record!"

"Yeah, that does suck," I deadpan. I can't help being sarcastic. Dave knows about my impending bankruptcy but he reacted to the news as if I said I had spilled black ink on my favorite dress or lost a brand new pair of shoes. Before I embarrass myself by opening that can of worms, I reach for my purse. "Can we wrap this up?"

Sandy quickly recaps what I suspected, that Beth is a new wife, not a stepparent. She doesn't say this in so many words, but she stresses that Dave and I should continue to communicate and coordinate all parental matters, and she thanks Beth for her openness and willingness to participate. Finally she reminds us that her door is always open if we'd like to come back as a group to navigate the housing transitions with the kids.

I leave with my head held high, puffed up and buoyed by my surge of assertiveness, but by the time I reach my car and settle into the driver's seat, which is hot from the sun, I'm beginning to wilt. I open the windows, pull forward into a spot of shade, and call Abigail.

"Mission accomplished. I laid down some rules and told them about my apartment."

"Good for you!"

We celebrate the clearing of this hurdle in our usual way, by recapping how far I've come and affirming that things always seem to work out.

"But will it ever really be over?" I hear the whine creeping into my voice. "I have these victories, and then some new challenge pops up."

"You can't help yourself, can you? Can you stay in gratitude for just a little while?"

I sigh. "You're right. I still feel like I have to be on guard."

"What you're describing is what happens when people get sober. It happened to a friend of mine. He kept saying, 'I'm so bored!' What feels boring or empty at first is actually just drama-free living."

"Hmm," I say, chewing on my fingernail. "I do like that idea."

"What if everything is okay right now? Just as it is."

Neither of us says anything, weighing this. I catch my eyes in the rear view mirror and consider this person that's me. We shoot each other a dubious look. What would it be like to stop looking backward?

That's when it happens. "Oh! I just heard a voice that wasn't mine."

"What did it say?" Abigail asks.

"It said, 'What if this is what freedom looks like?'"

The silence on the line is longer this time as those words settle.

"You need to write that on a piece of paper and put it on your wall," Abigail says finally, sounding exactly like my friend Suzie when she told me to post the reminder that Paul didn't even read my book. "That's your answer."

I drive home with this new idea of freedom riding shotgun. I have that awkward feeling of being in a car with a stranger, stealing shy and curious glances in an attempt to become acquainted. Is it possible that emptiness is actually space? That the unknown is in fact the doorway to pure potential? I think about my Healing Touch training, when the instructor replied to every question by shrugging and repeating, "Just ask." It annoyed me that our education was reduced to two simple words and that, rather than being given the answers, we were given the responsibility for our own learning. Now I see that there is no other way.

So I ask the only thing I can think to ask: "Show me." Show me my next step. Show me how to trust. Show me how to love.

Part Three

Meditate. Live purely. Be quiet. Do your work with mastery.
Like the moon, come out from behind the clouds. Shine!

—Buddha

29 Like the Moon

I begin at the beginning, with the tinkling of the ice cubes and the sloshing of scotch in a glass. I begin with Dave calling me to the table, and the way the hardwood floor tilted upward to catch me as I slid off my chair. I don't even look at what was scribbled in my journal. I just write, remembering every detail up until my knees hit the floor. But even that is the smallest gap in what is seared into my brain. Checking my journal for accuracy, I find that I've recreated our exchange verbatim.

When I'm finished I submit what I've written to a website for divorced moms. I know that if I put this story out in the world and proclaim that it's from an upcoming book, I'll be obligated to follow through, bound by the vicious worry of "what will they think?" if I don't deliver. As if there is ever a nameless, faceless, massive "they" waiting for the chance to judge us.

My chapter, now considered a blog, posts on what turns out to be a very active site with many visitors. Several days after it goes live, I open my email to find a message from the editor informing me that my piece has been picked up by the Huffington Post and reposted in their divorce section. She adds that it's been syndicated to the Australia and Germany editions as well, and includes links to all three.

I stare at the email for a few moments, my thoughts ricocheting between a sort of detached "Hmmm, how interesting," to "OH MY GOD, ARE YOU KIDDING ME?" I click on the links to find that the number of likes is already high and climbing. I call my friend Linda, also a writer, and thrill to the sound of her shrieking and hollering as if I've won the lottery. For a few blessed minutes it's easy to forget that the gory detonation of my marriage has been broadcast across the world.

Then I read some of the comments left by readers.

How stupid is this woman? reads one. *She's lying if she says she didn't know anything,* reads another. I relay these to Linda with a sick feeling in the back of my throat.

"Stop right there," she says. "You never read the comments. Those are written by mouth-breathers and bottom-feeders. Don't you know that?"

I didn't know that, but I'll take her word for it. She advises me to hire someone to pull out the positive remarks and deliver them to me like a party gift so I can reply to my supporters with a gracious and heartfelt thank you. Before the week is out, I've hired Carly's daughter to comb through the comments, now numbering over five hundred, while I focus on the number of likes the blog is getting as it reaches into the thousands.

Safeguarding myself in this way feels important, and just as I'm congratulating myself for growing thicker skin, a text appears on my phone. There's no name, just a number, but I know immediately who it's from. It's not Dave. It's Paul. *Why do you want to air dirty laundry? Why don't you just publish the book and be done with it?* Apparently it wasn't enough to delete Paul's name and messages, so I take the additional step of blocking him, not just from my phone, but from email and Facebook as well. I'm stung, but not completely surprised, by the meanness of his reproach. Then I marvel at his astounding lack of knowledge about being an author. He's imbued me with miraculous powers if he thinks I can "just publish" a book, lickety-split. In his words is an arrogant dismissiveness that's similar to the time Dave said he wanted to "wrap things up" with me in four weeks. Has Dave read my blog? I don't hear anything from him and have to assume that he hasn't. Of course it's only a matter of time before he sees it and discovers that I'm writing a book, but for now I allow myself to relax. The idea that I don't have to listen to what Dave or Paul or a stranger lurking behind a laptop thinks is revolutionary. So is the realization that I don't have to explain myself. The desire to make others understand me is deeply ingrained. As a teenager, when I first started writing short stories, my mother would read them and say, "Why do you have to write about such sad things? You think too deeply about everything."

I had no answer for my mom years ago, and I don't answer Paul or the haters either. I come to the conclusion that finding my voice sometimes includes remaining silent. For the first time, I give myself permission to think deeply, to feel deeply, and to keep writing.

I've always hated Mondays. It's not as if I have to get up early and head to an office, but I swear I can feel the collective heavy energy of all the people who loathe going back to work. On this particular Monday, Jed is complaining of a stomach ache, refusing to go to school. I decide that he has to go, even if he gets there late. He gets angry and starts to cry.

"What's wrong?" I ask for the third time, not really expecting an answer.

Finally he blurts, "I can't do it!"

A familiar stiffening takes place in my body as I go into resistance. I don't want to deal with this. Of my three children, Jed is the most enigmatic. He rarely articulates his thoughts or feelings, and uses touch rather than words to express himself. I understand his sensitivities, but don't always like them. Right now I wish he knew how to keep it together, or at least explain how he's feeling so I can do something about it.

Wow. There's an irony. I want both of us to be allowed to feel deeply, except when it's inconvenient. I begin to cry with him, saddened by the existence of this hard edge in me that wants to push him to do what I think he "should" do. I pray for help, but I hear nothing.

Maybe *nothing* is the answer. The teacher in my Deepening class said, "When you don't know what to do, do nothing." So Jed and I sit, arms around one another, until our tears turn to sniffles. I remember saying the same words as Jed—*I can't do it!*—when I was in labor with him, and the way the midwife quietly pointed out, "You *are* doing it."

After a while I say, "We're going to give it a try. I'm going to drive you to school, and I'll stay in the neighborhood, and your teacher can call me if you need me." I'm amazed that he doesn't rage. He cries again, a sad, resigned cry, but lets me put on his shoes. I give him a bag of popcorn for the car and deliver him to school without further incident.

When I pick him up at the end of the day he comes out smiling.

"My teacher told me that it takes a bright shiny person to come when he's not feeling well," he says.

"Like a lighthouse," I say. "They don't run around saving ships. They do nothing but shine."

He grins, and for a moment we both feel it: we're going to shine.

There are 178 steps to the top of the Tybee Island Lighthouse in Georgia. I'm halfway up when I pause to look out a small square window and immediately wish I hadn't. Vertigo makes me wobble. I want to go back down. But Carly is behind me and we've promised each other we'll push through our fear of heights for one quick bird's-eye glimpse of the Atlantic Ocean.

Though Carly and I have been friends since birth, we've never gone on a vacation together. Now, since Dave has the kids again for spring break, I wanted to make sure I wouldn't be wallowing in loneliness or pining for the days when I played house with Paul. I arranged another house swap for a lovely condo just steps from the beach on this charming island thirty miles from Savannah, trading the damp and dirty monochrome of the city for the instant color and heat of the South. Carly and her husband Kevin are here, along with a couple of friends I've met more recently, since the divorce, at the spiritual center I attend. They don't know Dave, and this adds to my sense of freedom.

Back on terra firma with shaky knees and parched throats after braving the lighthouse, we decide to drive into Savannah in search of cool drinks and a gluten-free bakery. Kevin drives, with Carly beside him in the front, and I share the back seat with my friend George. My phone rings. It's a Healing Touch colleague calling with questions about homework for our certification requirements. We chat about that, and then she surprises me by saying that she just ordered my novel after another colleague told her about it.

Hanging up, I say to the others, "She didn't know that I'm an author."

George snorts. "*Author* is a pretty broad term."

I'm stung. Kevin jumps to my defense. "She did write a book," he says pointedly.

"And she's writing another one now," Carly adds.

It's time to defend myself. I turn to face George squarely. "What *exactly* was that supposed to mean?"

He squirms and says, "It was a joke."

"How could anyone consider that funny?"

"Sorry," he says with a sheepish shrug and a tone that seems to say *jeez, lay off*, as if he's the injured party. That's when I make a vow to myself: I'll no longer allow anyone into my life who doesn't honor or see me for who I am.

That night, sitting alone beside the ocean, I'm still hurt by George's words. Why do I continue to be around men who belittle me? I thought I left that behind. As if to affirm it, I walk along the shore as the waves break and bellow at my feet. There's a full moon hanging fat and low in the starless sky, making the shoreline glow with an eerie brightness. I walk until I see a rowboat resting, useless, in the tall grass. It's warped and peeling and forlorn. I hear the words of a song that was written for the TV show *Nashville*: "What if you're just a vessel? And God gave you something special? It ain't yours to throw away."

In my last therapy session with Walter, after I complained about all the circumstances and people who steal writing time from me, about how I'm overwhelmed and unsupported and don't know how to reach my goals, he shrugged and simply said, "A writer writes."

Another simple answer. Just not an easy one.

When I return to Chicago a miracle has started unfolding, first in the form of forsythia, then magnolia, spirea, and lilac. It's a progression that occurs predictably every year, but fills me with surprise and wonder each time. The transformation from lifeless concrete frozen beneath dull, heavy skies to a vibrant frenzy of green is nothing short of lifesaving.

I dump my suitcase on the floor, make myself a cup of tea, and grab a week's worth of mail from the front foyer. There's an envelope from my lawyer Scott. Inside is a court document. Dave has filed a cease and desist motion to stop me from writing my book. My first instinct is to lunge for the phone to call Scott for assurance—this is ridiculous, right?—but I resist the urge. I've been through enough with him and the Cook County court system to know that he'll tell me when and if I need to worry.

Instead I call Abigail. "You won't believe this. . . ." I begin.

Of course she does believe it. What's more, she's not surprised. I realize that neither am I. Instead, what I feel is . . . *space*. I know that's not a feeling, but it's a sensation surrounding me that allows me to breathe and intentionally choose not to react.

Scott never calls about the motion. I'm not required to be anywhere or do anything, and the threat of a gag order magically fades, as if it never happened. The only reminder of it comes a few weeks later, when my brother Bryan calls to say that he talked to Dave.

"Uh oh." I hold my breath. Bryan hasn't spoken to Dave since before this all began. He's had plenty of choice words *about* Dave, but no contact.

"He wants me to make you stop writing your book," Bryan says.

I groan. "What did you say?"

There's a long pause. "I politely declined. Let's leave it at that."

And so we do.

A person's handwriting is as unique as a fingerprint. When I see my name written in Dave's hand on an envelope in my mailbox, it's as familiar to me as his face. And as personal. I steel myself as if he were there in the flesh, noting how strange it is that, after the judge, and then my brother, I'm the last person he's appealing to. As I hold it in my hand, it's almost like I have X-ray vision. That's how certain I am about what's inside. Dave will explain why I can't write a book about my life. He'll write things like *I know you don't want to.* . . .

But Dave doesn't know what I want. For so long, I didn't either.

Now I do. So instead of reading it, I put it, unopened, in a drawer, on top of the note from Suzie reminding me that Paul "DIDN'T EVEN READ YOUR BOOK." Somewhere else, in some other drawer, is my letter to Paul, full of its own pleas and manipulations.

I'm done with appeals. I'd rather put my words in a book. Not to convince anyone of anything, but because my story matters to the only one I can control: me.

30 The Table Is Set

Oh, it's a beauty—long enough to seat eight people, it's made of Brazilian bamboo, with an espresso finish—a style I would call transitional; not as rustic as a farmhouse table, but not modern either. And it's sturdy. No more wobble.

The two men who deliver the table stand by patiently as I eyeball its position, making sure it's perfectly centered in my new dining room.

"Nice place," one of them says approvingly.

"Yeah, thanks." I feel myself beaming. I think of Jed and how he worried about moving. In the house, the boys slept in a basement bedroom, on a different floor from me. When I told Jed we were moving he said he wanted a bedroom next to mine. In this apartment my bedroom is the middle one, with the boys' bedroom on one side of me and April's on the other. It may be a small and unsurprising detail, but it pleases me to think that Jed's prayers are being answered the same way mine have been.

"Are you from Michigan?" the mover asks, pointing to a plaque on the wall that says *Lake Michigan: Unsalted.*

I say yes and learn that he's also a Michigander. As we continue to chat, we discover that we both went to the same high school in Jackson, a small, centrally located city known for its federal prison.

I love these kinds of coincidences and the accompanying thrill that follows. I once heard a spiritual teacher describe it like this: "When all that *is* responds to us and becomes personal, that's God."

Recognizing God becomes like a game. During a long afternoon of driving the kids to various activities, I pop an audiobook in the car stereo. It's actor Rob Lowe's biography, *Stories I Only Tell My Friends,* and Logan and I are enjoying his story about how, as a kid, he tried to meet Telly Savalas. I have to pause the disc to explain that Telly Savalas was the star of a 1970s cop show called *Kojak,* and that his character always had a lollipop in his mouth. Rob describes how he gave a lollipop to Mr. Savalas' assistant, and in the next breath, he uses the term "slippery slope" to describe his mother's deteriorating marriage.

"Hey!" Jed interjects from the back seat, where he's been reading. "My book is called *Slippery Slope!*" Seconds later he pipes up again, "Whoa! Listen to this." He reads a line about a lollipop.

These doses of divine magic continue to occur, though they aren't always lighthearted. One chilly, rainy morning I pull up in front of a Starbucks to get coffee and notice a woman sitting on a bench outside, shrieking. Cars are passing, their drivers rubbernecking, while people on the sidewalk look away. I hesitate before getting out of my car, disturbed but fascinated by the racket she's making. I think of Edvard Munch's painting, *The Scream.* I know what it's like to want to let out a primal cry. Mixed with my concern for her is a tinge of admiration that she's doing it. Then, as I wait to cross the street, I hear a watery sound and the pavement beneath her darkens as she releases a stream of urine. She needs help. But her hysterics are frightening and I'm not sure what to do. Should I call the police, who can call social services? I rush into the Starbucks and order a coffee and a sandwich. My total comes to $9.11. Thankful for the guidance, I call 911 and wait on the sidewalk until the police come to gently lead her away.

What's the purpose of these mystical moments? All I know is that they remind me I'm not alone. When Dave read me the three things on his list, shattering the scaffold I called my life, and then did nothing when I fell to the floor, a void opened that made me question if I had ever existed at all. Divine magic reminds me that not only do I exist, but that I matter. Even when it leaves me baffled, there's a kernel of knowingness inherent in it.

There's also a sense that I'm participating in life, not at its mercy. As I sit at my new table, running my hand along the cool smooth surface, I have to admit that life is starting to look more like a table spread with dishes I've had a hand in preparing. Years ago, when I attended a Methodist church, my favorite part of the service was at the end, during communion, when the pastor would raise her arms and say, "The table is set, won't you come?"

At this table I say yes to the invitation, and give thanks for something as simple as a cup of tea.

At this table I remember the way the congregation would form a line and, with outstretched hands, receive the bread of life, singing: *Praise God, from whom all blessings flow. . . .*

At this table I count my blessings, and wait for my teachers to arrive. Silence and solitude are the main ones. I access them through meditation; they show me yawning horizons of spaciousness and little sips of freedom. I await my children too—Logan who channels wisdom beyond his years; Jed, who channeled an otherworldly force of nature when he was born and shows me how to swim against the stream; April, whose copper hair and melodious voice remind me that happiness doesn't come from seeing my likeness replicated, but from seeing a wondrous emanation of God that is wholly apart from me.

They remind me of my place. I'm not frightfully small, but humbled. Outside the window of my new apartment, I see a pattern of leaves dancing on the wall of the building across the street. It's a mesmerizing image, the way it shifts and changes, fades and returns, depending on the angle of the sun. I could watch it for hours. The leaves appear tangible even though there's nothing there but projection. Is it the shadow that makes it beautiful? Or the light?

I need them both.

It's a small round table covered with a white silk cloth that sits between me and a Dutch woman named Anneke. She's telling me that she recently moved to Chicago from Amsterdam to teach art at Columbia College. We're on the second floor of a beautiful brownstone in the Wicker Park neighborhood of Chicago, at an upscale salon that offers body and soul services—everything from hair-care and massage to energy sessions, crystal healing, and oracle card readings. After being a stay-at-home mom for almost eight years, I've earned my certification as a Healing Touch practitioner and have been hired to work part time as an Intuitive Healer. I'm older and far less stylish than most of the staff, who wear rumpled, mismatched thrift store finds that inexplicably look more put together than my permanent press dresses and solid cardigans.

Life has inexplicably brought me to a healing sanctuary. That's what the second floor is officially called. It's a light and spacious haven, a place of soothing music and hushed tones. One wall holds all the best-selling metaphysical and spiritual books I could ask for, and I read them between clients. I search their pages for insights about how to deal with Dave, who continues to feel like a stranger to me. He never brings up the cease and desist motion, or the letter he wrote me. He seems to switch gears so easily, making me wonder if Logan was right when he said, "No offense, Mom, but Dad is better at this stuff than you are."

My new job includes doing Angel Card readings for the clients, something I've done for myself but never "professionally." I'm relieved to discover that it doesn't involve mind-reading or prognostication. I find that when I relax and allow myself to speak without editing myself, the messages that come through are meaningful to my clients. I begin each session by asking "What area of your life would you most like to see improved? Where do you need some clarity?" I notice that even when the client answers career or finances, the cards often point toward romantic relationships. The real question is always: will I be loved?

It's a colossal cosmic joke that anyone is looking to *me* for an answer to this question. I can only hope that what I lack in knowledge, I make up for in my ability to relate to the fear and longing behind the question. One thing is certain—each session works to heal me, too, as I hear myself telling my clients things that I also need to hear.

Anneke tells me she's struggling with a constant sense of imbalance between teaching art and creating her own art. She complains that she doesn't have enough time in the day to teach, be creative, exercise, and practice self-care.

"But what if this is your rhythm?" I ask. "So you didn't do all that in one day. But you told me you had an art installation last month. You taught a class yesterday. You rode your bike here today and you're having a massage after our session. What if it takes you twenty-four days to cycle through your goals, instead of twenty-four hours?"

Anneke looks surprised. I'm beginning to see a pattern with many people, including myself. We don't stop to acknowledge our accomplishments or to honor our own processes. Before I give Anneke my card I write on the back: *Comparison is the killer of joy.* When she leaves, I ask myself the same question: What if I'm following my own rhythm for healing? I may not be "good at" hiding my feelings and acting friendly when I'm angry and hurt. It may take me longer than Dave to let go, but, as I remind myself, Dave had ten years of "letting go."

Soon after, life brings me another lesson in the form of a tall, good-looking firefighter who is waiting for me at the beginning of my shift. I don't have a chance to prepare myself the way I'd like; I'm even more unprepared for his tears. As soon as I look at him, he begins sobbing.

"I cheated on my wife," he says, swiping roughly at his eyes. "I keep trying to apologize but she won't listen. She won't talk to me. I know she's gonna leave me."

My heart drops. Why me? How can I have compassion for this man? How can I help?

I take a deep breath and remind myself that I'm not in charge here. As I invite Spirit to take the lead, I look into his eyes and listen to his outpouring of pain. When it subsides he asks plaintively, "What do I do? What do I do?"

I tell him the only thing I know. "You have to let her have her experience. Let her be angry on *her* timetable, not yours. Be willing to listen to what it's like for her. Show her you're sorry by asking what *she* needs."

"But I have to *do* something." He looks like he's going to jump out of the chair. If an inferno erupted in this three-story Victorian brownstone, he would tackle it single-handedly.

"Do nothing. Just listen, and wait."

I walk him to the door of the healing sanctuary and watch his broad back, rounded with grief, as it disappears down the long staircase. From the second-floor window I see him hesitate on the busy sidewalk, and I wonder which way he'll turn. I hope his wife, whoever she is, is allowed to light up the sky with her rage and that this man can watch the flames without rushing to quench them. I hope she can be heard. I hope her anger is strong enough to purify and transform and forgive.

I hope love wins.

31 Learning to Dance

D ave and Beth are married. They're now a picture-perfect couple, so much so that they've been photographed for the cover of *Crain's Chicago Business* magazine. They're featured in an article about how stepparents are either relegated to support status or simply invisible. But Beth isn't invisible. She's posed with Dave and my kids on the front steps of their house, as if she's lived there for more than two months, as if she's been mothering my children for years. She's being interviewed because she started a support group for other women like her.

"There was an air of relief for all of us," she's quoted as saying about their first support meeting. "Somebody gets it!"

I'm glad somebody gets Beth. I'm even glad Beth gets Dave. And I'm okay with not understanding any of it. Like the poet Rilke advised, I'm learning to accept life's questions as if they're locked rooms or books written in a foreign language. What other choice is there? Ralph Waldo Emerson said, "All is riddle, and the key to a riddle is another riddle."

This makes me remember something Dave and I shared. Years earlier, we used to enjoy asking friends the riddle about albatross soup: A man walks into a restaurant and orders albatross soup. He takes one bite and then kills himself. Why?

Through a series of yes or no answers, most people are able to arrive at the answer. The man is a sailor who was shipwrecked with his crewmates. Some died of starvation, but the captain kept the rest alive by feeding them what he called "albatross soup." After he is rescued, the sailor orders albatross soup at a restaurant, but when he tastes it, he realizes it was *not* albatross soup he'd eaten before. He had eaten the flesh of his dead crewmates. He kills himself because he can't forgive himself.

As I sit in my new apartment on the day of Dave's wedding, unpacking the last of my moving boxes, I can't help wondering what Dave and Beth have together. This leads to remembering what we had. I try to conjure some vestige of the feelings I once felt for Dave in the early days, before the kids. What remains most real is the memory of friendship. What still hurts most is the loss of that. No series of questions and answers will lead me to understand whether that was simply not enough. And suddenly the riddle of the albatross soup takes on another meaning when I admit something painful: It wasn't until I tasted the love I felt for Paul that I realized I never had that with Dave. Of course I loved him, but it was a love that came from my head more than my heart. Perhaps Dave knew that. And wouldn't that leave him hungry? While I'll never approve or understand Dave's choices, I now believe that *he believed* his actions weren't affecting me. Like the captain, Dave was deceitful, but maybe his actions were desperate attempts to keep us alive.

Maybe, in our completely different ways, we were trying to survive the only way we knew how.

I stand on the edge of the dance floor at a North Side studio called May I Have This Dance? Abigail has brought me to one of their weekly dance parties, and I'm watching couples glide, spin, and triple-step as they do the West Coast Swing. The tempo of the music is fast, but the beating of my heart is faster. I want to dance, but I'm afraid I'm not good enough.

The song ends, and as another begins, a white-haired gentleman with a rakish smile offers me his hand and pulls me onto the floor, waving away my protests that I'm only a beginner.

Okay. If he can do this, so can I.

I manage to find a respectable groove, but whenever he tries to lead me in anything other than the basic steps, I stumble. All I can do is smile a lot and apologize even more. I need to let myself be led and this is much more frightening and challenging than I expected.

After I've mumbled "*sorry*" for the tenth time, he laughs and says, "It's okay. You're blonde."

Huh? It's delivered like a compliment, so I decide to take it as one; if I can't be graceful, I can at least be gracious. But later, after the shoes have come off and I'm in my own quiet room, his words keep dancing through my head.

Do I act blonde? If you believe the stereotype, blondes are assumed to be helpless, shallow, unambitious, or naive. Of course I know these traits have nothing to do with hair color. Still, something in this idea strikes a nerve. Why do I apologize so much? In what ways do I minimize myself and my efforts? And the big one: How seriously do I take myself?

As an experiment, I promptly dye my hair brown and discover that I feel plainer, duller, and more average with darker hair. I also feel more thoughtful, more discerning, more earnest. I decide to get serious about having fun. The last time I took dance lessons was with Dave before our wedding. We spent weeks learning a choreographed foxtrot to a single song for our reception. Wouldn't it be fun to be able to dance to any song, with any partner? I check out the class offerings at the studio. The registration deadline is fast approaching and I can't decide between West Coast Swing, East Coast Swing,

Country Two-Step, or Hustle. While I'm considering my options, I have a conversation with a friend and he begins telling me a story about life lessons he learned in his twenties.

"I had to learn to hustle," he says.

His words provide the answer I need. Hustle it is! The next morning, driving my kids to school along a different route than usual, I'm waiting at a traffic light when the Hustle dance instructor walks in front of my car. I smile and thank God for showing me the steps to take.

The next three months fly by as I advance through four levels of group dance lessons until I finally know the steps and can hold my own.

Soon after, I'm back on the dance floor when the same white-haired man grabs me. At first he doesn't recognize me. Once he does, he says, "Okay, now you've got to work it. Give me some attitude!"

I smile, not missing a beat as he leads me through a sugar push turn. I feel an inner diva come to life, and her power doesn't come from the color of her hair. She invites me to surrender to the music, and I follow because she is weightless, and free, and alive.

32 My Word

Imagine an angel perched on a mountaintop, wearing a suit of golden feathers, framed by a flowing purple robe, majestic wings, and billowy rainbow clouds. Her arm is raised, beckoning. This is the oracle card I keep pulling, again and again. It says *Hello from Heaven,* and the angel it depicts is Archangel Azrael. The message reads: *Your loved ones in heaven are doing fine. Let go of worries, and feel their loving blessings.* Why do I keep getting this card? I wonder if it refers to my dad, but if this is supposed to be a message from him, I'm confused.

Over the course of several days, I continue to pull the same card. Each time I feel equally baffled. After the third time, I leave the card lying on my desk.

Passing by later, I glance at the desk and three words float from the card as if penned in phosphorous: *Hello. Loved. Ones.* It's the name of my novel. I grab the oracle deck and flip through each card to see if any other one has these three words on it, in any combination. None of them do.

Hello Loved Ones. If it's a message about my novel, what does it mean? And is it connected to my dad? For all I know, he didn't even finish reading it. He just left me hanging.

I feel a pang of guilt: I left my characters hanging too. The people in my novel were real to me. They spoke to me, sharing their deepest secrets and darkest fears. They allowed me to create them; by stepping onto the page they gave me the gift of expressing myself. And then, when they were ready to be seen and heard, I stuffed them away in a drawer. I never gave them the debut they deserved. Truman Capote said finishing a book is just like taking a child out in the backyard and shooting it. I did something else: I let it languish. I broke the trust I had put into my vision.

Listening to a Unity radio program one morning, I hear these words: No one else can betray us unless we first betray ourselves.

I put the Archangel Azrael card in my purse—for luck, or courage—grab my keys, and head out the front door. I walk the five blocks to the local bookstore where, thanks to an unseasonably warm day, the door is propped open, providing easy access to something I wanted to do long ago.

"Is the owner in?" I ask the girl behind the counter.

When he comes over I introduce myself and ask if I can reserve the store for an event. A book signing. We discuss details and dates, and with ease and grace this small step expands into what feels like a tap dance around my heart. He gives me a handshake and a smile that I decide is angelic; before I leave I look around the space and see myself standing at the front of the room. I can't help comparing this vision to the night Dave staged my play, when I sat in the audience, a spectator to my own creation, an observer rather than participant.

As I walk home, I think about hope and expectation. They're like two friends who have captivated and entertained me all these years, but never really offered anything. If I'm writing a new script—this time just for me—then I can choose new words. I *choose* to replace hope and expectation with faith and intention. Actor Jim Carrey, in a commencement speech he gave at Maharishi University, said, "Hope is a beggar. Hope walks through the fire, faith leaps over it."

I'm ready to leap.

I'm back at Open Books, this time volunteering as a writing coach. A yellow bus pulls up and a group of rowdy kids from a South Side school fills the room. My job is to sit with a table of six preteens and help them write stories based on photos. One girl creates a successful woman who lives in New York City, works at the United Nations, hates pineapple, and wears mismatched socks. One boy describes his professional basketball career and the house that he will buy for his grandmother, complete with trash compactor and a Jacuzzi tub with grab bars. Another boy goes into such elaborate detail about how much he loves spicy chicken wings from KFC that our mouths begin watering.

All the kids, even the shy ones, are quick to share, and there is a lot of hooting and hollering and back-slapping as they support one another. At the end of the workshop, we raise our pencils and shout at the top of our lungs, "I am an author! I have something to say!" I get goose bumps. I think back to the first time I was here, with Jed's class, and how worried I was that he was not fully participating. I wasn't fully participating either, in my marriage, or my faith, or my work. But I'm so grateful for that day when Jed stood up to share his poem about me because I learned something about creating character. I learned that it doesn't matter what the story is, as long as it's your own, and you tell it for yourself, no matter what anyone else thinks.

We all shout those words one more time, "I am an author!"

Why is it true? *Because I say so.*

Epilogue: What We Most Want

The gym is packed with parents craning and waving to the mass of kids who sit criss-cross-applesauce in front of the stage. The holiday show hasn't yet begun, but cell phones flash, capturing blurry photos that are destined to be deleted.

I'll be lucky to get a seat. I scan the rows of folding chairs and there is Dave, with an empty seat beside him. He's alone and he waves me over. Taking a deep breath, I squeeze past snow boots and knees draped with down jackets to sit beside him. We chat about the stage decorations and about how tall April has gotten. We chat about Christmas, just two weeks away.

Outwardly, it's only a conversation. Inside me, it's something new. I'm not rehashing the past. I'm not worrying about the future. There's an awareness that to be here in this moment is to be a woman sitting in a chair watching what unfolds. This is freedom. This is peace.

That night, at home, April pulls a piece of yellow construction paper from her school folder. "You have to share this with Daddy," she says as she proudly presents it to me. She's made a drawing of what looks like a lumpy vase with handles. Under it, she's written:

Mom and Dadyy win the trofye.

Wow! Ceap it up! Youv done a asum job!

I give her a hug before sticking it on the refrigerator. Later, after I drive the kids to Dave's and I'm alone in the quiet house, wrapped in a fuzzy pink bathrobe, I'll take it down, fold it carefully, and tuck it into one of my favorite books, *Other Voices, Other Rooms* by Truman Capote, to be discovered again one day. I'll put it on top of my favorite passage:

What we most want is only to be held . . . and told . . . that everything (everything is a funny thing, is baby milk and Papa's eyes, is roaring logs on a cold morning, is hoot-owls and the boy who makes you cry after school, is Mama's long hair, is being afraid and twisted faces on the bedroom wall) . . . everything is going to be all right.

And so it is.

A Letter From Tammy Letherer

Dear Reader,

I will never forget the flash of insight I had the day I finished this book. It was a crisp, clear October day, the kind that is perfectly poised between letting go and preparing to harvest. I was walking home from Starbucks, having just typed the words I had been struggling toward for years: The End.

In that moment I knew two things. First, that what I wanted was to be the book in your lap that lets you know you are not alone. I hope that whatever situation you're facing, however difficult it may be, you will feel the truth of that—you are never alone, the universe is conspiring for your good, and, as unlikely as it sometimes seems, you can *always* interpret events in your favor.

My second insight was knowing that I had to help others experience the same satisfaction I was feeling after completing a project that often felt insurmountable. Nothing compares to the peace that comes with expressing yourself the best way you possibly can, to coming as close to your truth as you are able and, in the process, feeling free. That was the day I committed to being a writing coach.

So thank you for reading this book and being part of my journey. If you enjoyed it I would be so grateful if you would post a review. If you would like to stay connected, please consider signing up for my newsletter. And if I can help you write your own story and find even a sliver of peace, I would love to hear from you.

All the best,
Tammy Letherer

www.TammyLetherer.com
@TLetherer
Facebook/TammyLetherer

Acknowledgements

Thanks to all the angels whose love and support helped me keep my eyes on the horizon, and whose acts of kindness, large and small, carried me through.

There's no one better in a crisis than V. I could not have made it through without your Taurus gifts, in particular your voice of reason and eye for beauty.

I'm grateful to Eric for keeping my heart open while I found my way back to myself.

Thank you Mike Lohman, Noelle McWard, and Chelle Van Wassenhove for opening your homes to me and my children and for being the kind of friends who accept me wherever I am, from puddle to princess.

Dr. Larry Stoler, Katie Huff Oberlin, Barry Paul Price, and Ann Sedgwick provided wisdom, insight, and clarity that lit my way. The hospitality and kindness of Patty and Jay Whitehouse brightened one of my darkest hours.

Joni VanRhee and Michelle Schnorr, words haven't been invented to convey what decades have created. BFF are the letters that come the closest. I love you both.

Thanks first, last, and always to my mother, my sister, and my brothers.

I appreciate my newsletter subscribers for their patience in the prolonged birthing of this book and for continuing to follow me whether I'm blogging about divorce, parenting, spirituality, writing, or any minutia in between.

Pat Verducci is an amazing story coach who pushed me to places I didn't really want to go—thank you! I'm grateful for my beta readers, Kate Flynn, Katy Boyce, Rose Mattax, Sandy Suminski, Suzanne Bayramian, and to Brooke Warner and the entire team at She Writes Press.

To the most powerful vision-holder I know, my prayer partner Danny Faith, thank you for your constant reminders that "It's all good in God's neighborhood."

Finally, I'm grateful for Bodhi Spiritual Center and its mission to reveal love, honor all paths, and celebrate life. The New Thought community has lifted me higher than any horizon I could have imagined.

*"Your final emancipation will be written by your own hand
or it will never be written at all; it will be thought
out by your own mind."*

—Ernest Holmes

About the Author

© Rose Yuen

Tammy Letherer is a writing coach, blogger, and author of the novel *Hello Loved Ones*. She lives in Chicago with her children and enjoys yoga, swing dancing, reading a good novel, Earl Grey tea, and spending time outdoors. Visit her at TammyLetherer.com.

SELECTED TITLES FROM SHE WRITES PRESS

She Writes Press is an independent publishing company
founded to serve women writers everywhere.
Visit us at www.shewritespress.com.

Loveyoubye: Holding Fast, Letting Go, And Then There's The Dog
by Rossandra White. $16.95, 978-1-938314-50-6.
A soul-searching memoir detailing the painful, but ultimately liberating,
disintegration of a twenty-five-year marriage.

The Full Catastrophe: A Memoir
by Karen Elizabeth Lee. $16.95, 978-1-63152-024-2.
The story of a well educated, professional woman who, after marrying
the wrong kind of man—twice—finally resurrects her life.

Not Exactly Love: A Memoir
by Betty Hafner. $16.95, 978-1-63152-149-2.
At twenty-five Betty Hafner thought she'd found the man to make her
dream of a family and cozy home come true—but after they married, his
rages turned the dream into a nightmare, and Betty had to decide: stay
with the man she loved, or find a way to leave?

Seeing Red: A Woman's Quest for Truth, Power, and the Sacred
by Lone Morch. $16.95, 978-1-938314-12-4.
One woman's journey over inner and outer mountains—a quest that
takes her to the holy Mt. Kailas in Tibet, through a seven-year marriage,
and into the arms of the fierce goddess Kali, where she discovers her
powerful, feminine self.

There Was a Fire Here: A Memoir
by Risa Nye. $16.95, 978-1-63152-045-7.
After a devastating firestorm destroys Risa Nye's Oakland, California home
and neighborhood, she has to dig deep to discover her inner strength and
resilience.

*Falling Together: How to Find Balance, Joy, and Meaningful Change
When Your Life Seems to be Falling Apart*
by Donna Cardillo. $16.95, 978-1-63152-077-8.
A funny, big-hearted self-help memoir that tackles divorce, caregiv-
ing, burnout, major illness, fears, and low self-esteem—and explores the
renewal that comes when we are able to meet these challenges with courage.